MARCO POLO

CELEBRATING FIFTY GOLDEN YEARS
OF OCEAN TRAVEL

RICHARD CLAMMER

ISBN 978-1-906608-88-0
Designed and produced by Ferry Publications,
a trading name of Lily Publications Ltd
PO Box 33, Ramsey, Isle of Man IM99 4LP
Tel +44 (0) 1624 898446   Fax +44 (0) 1624 898449
Email info@lilypublications.co.uk
www.lilypublications.co.uk

Ferry
Publications

Cruise & Maritime Voyages
Head Office
Gateway House, Stonehouse Lane
Purfleet, Essex RM19 1NS
United Kingdom
Tel: (0044) 01708 893 100
www.cruiseandmaritime.com

CONTENTS

Foreword 3

1   Enter the Russian Poets 5

2   Alexandr Pushkin, the Soviet Years 15

3   Marco Polo, from Poet to Explorer 37

4   The Advent of Cruise & Maritime Voyages 45

5   Marco Polo Today 65

Timeline 88

Acknowledgements & References 90

Technical Information 91

Marco Polo's CMV Masters and Chief Engineers 91

CMV Voyage List 92

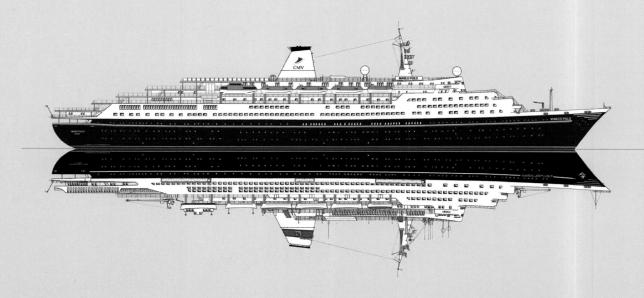

FOREWORD

The *Marco Polo* is indeed a remarkable ship with a proud and fascinating history spanning an amazing fifty years of ocean going travel.

Marco Polo, which was originally built in 1965, was purchased by our group of companies in 2007 and we feel privileged to be the custodians of this truly iconic vessel. From the moment we first visited *Marco Polo* we all knew she was rather special!

The year 1991 was a pivotal one for the *Marco Polo* when, as *Alexandr Pushkin,* she was acquired by British shipping entrepreneur, Gerry Herrod and his Group. The vessel was completely rebuilt in Greece and renamed *Marco Polo* operating under the Orient Lines brand. This massive investment and high quality refit set the scene for many more years of service by this fine vessel.

Today *Marco Polo* continues to have a huge following and is much loved and adored by thousands of regular passengers. We believe this is testament to her classic and traditional style, stunning lines and layout, and the special ambience and charisma which she exudes. Her dedicated and hardworking international officers and crew, many of whom have stayed with us since we started operations in 2008, really appreciate the significance of serving on board this very special lady and contribute hugely to her success.

Behind the scenes we have a dedicated team of specialist technicians, engineers, mariners, hotel managers and staff at our ship management offices in Greece and other international locations. Taking care of such a fine and elegant ship requires meticulous planning and preparation starting with her annual docking in November, ensuring that every minute detail is covered and that she is ready again for the commencement of each fresh new season.

Looking back at her remarkable career, *Marco Polo* has probably covered more nautical miles and visited more ports of call than virtually any other cruise liner afloat today, and is still powered by her original main engines. Over the past fifty years *Marco Polo* has sailed the seven seas across the globe and, apart from sailing extensively throughout Europe, she has journeyed to Antarctica and the Arctic Polar Regions, the Galapagos Islands, Amazonia, North & South America, Africa, the Far East, Australasia and the Pacific.

Marco Polo's 50th anniversary year in 2015 heralds a very special and exciting golden anniversary cruise programme to mark this memorable achievement, reached by very few other cruise liners. The pinnacle of the cruise calendar is *Marco Polo's* epic 36 night commemorative voyage to Canada and Greenland sailing from London Tilbury. This unique voyage retraces part of her regular transatlantic liner service from Leningrad, Bremerhaven, Tilbury and Le Havre to Montreal and back. In all, she completed nearly forty such voyages between 1967 and 1971.

We look forward to welcoming back regular passengers and new guests alike during 2015 to join us in the birthday celebration of this very special lady.

This special commemorative book plots *Marco Polo's* amazing life story in great detail and draws together a wonderful collection of historic and modern illustrations. It is a fitting tribute to this wonderful ship and a celebration of her fifty golden years of ocean travel.

Nikolaos Tragakes
Chairman
Global Maritime Group

Ivan Franko, the first ship of the 'Russian Poet' class, at speed in the English Channel, showing her striking original livery and the 1974 extension of her forward superstructure. (FotoFlite)

ENTER THE RUSSIAN POETS

In the field of international relations, the 1960s will be remembered as the most dangerous and glacial period in the Cold War between the Soviet Union and the West. 1961, the year in which John F. Kennedy was elected President of the United States, was marked by the abortive US-backed Bay of Pigs invasion of Cuba, the construction of the Berlin Wall, the beginning of the stand-off between Soviet and U.S. tanks at Checkpoint Charlie and the USSR's resumption of testing nuclear devices in the atmosphere. A year later, in October 1962, the Cuban Missile Crisis brought the world to the very brink of nuclear war.

It was in this context that, early in 1962, the Soviet Merchant Marine Ministry passenger ship division, Morskoi Passazhirskogo Flot, (MORPASFLOT) placed an order for the construction of the first three of a new class of 19,860 gross ton liners with V.E.B. Mathias Thesen Werft of Wismar in East Germany. A further batch of three was ordered in the spring of 1964 although only two were actually completed. Instead of building the final ship, the Soviets purchased the larger, 24,981 gross ton West German liner *Hamburg* which was renamed *Maksim Gorkiy*. The MORPASFLOT fleet was managed by fifteen different Soviet shipping companies the largest of which, The Baltic Steamship Company and the Black Sea Shipping Company, were designated as operators of the new liners although strategic policy and central control remained firmly with the ministry – MORFLOT – in Moscow.

The new ships were intended both for cruising and to fulfil a stated Soviet aim to establish a regular liner service between Leningrad (St. Petersburg) and New York, calling at a variety of western European ports en route. Although strained US/Soviet relations, which precluded any immediate possibility of the New York service commencing, may have made the timing of the order appear somewhat illogical, it did in fact fit perfectly with the Soviet thinking of the time.

Since the death of Stalin in 1953 the Soviet merchant fleet had grown rapidly, doubling in size between 1945 and 1960, and redoubling again in the next five years. The enormous length of the Soviet Union's coastline (over 40,000kms/25,000 miles, facing two oceans and twelve seas), combined with the relative lack of rail and road networks, meant that seagoing transport remained the only efficient means of moving bulk goods, particularly to the isolated communities of the north and far east. An extensive and flexible domestic passenger and cargo fleet was therefore essential.

In addition, the expansion of foreign trade was a central aim of Soviet foreign policy. With the Baltic Sea ports giving ready access to the Atlantic, the Arctic Ocean seaboard to both the Atlantic and Pacific, and the Black Sea providing an outlet to the Mediterranean there was certainly no shortage of available sea lanes and by the mid 1960s it was estimated that Soviet merchant vessels were calling at over 800 ports in 90 different countries. Quite apart from supplying the Soviet Union's import needs, this extensive foreign trade was seen as essential for several key reasons. Firstly, and most straightforwardly, it provided MORFLOT with much needed foreign hard currency, and secondly, it enabled the USSR to expand her global sphere of influence by pouring billions of pounds worth of economic and military aid into non-aligned 'Third World' countries such as Angola, Egypt and others, as well as into its own East-European satellite states.

Over and above these vital economic/trade functions, the Soviet government regarded its merchant fleet as a vital fourth arm of its defence forces. In the case of a military operation being launched against one of its European neighbours or a more distant adversary, it was planned that large numbers of merchant vessels would be requisitioned to act as troop ships or transports and provide other logistical support for the military. For this reason, many new vessels within the expanding merchant fleet were built with higher speed, endurance and heavy cargo capacity than might be expected for purely civilian use.

Finally, the presence of Soviet vessels in ports all around the world gave a golden opportunity for intelligence gathering and it was widely assumed that many of them were fitted with sophisticated electronic listening equipment and had naval specialists within their civilian crews.

For all of these reasons, the 1960s saw a herculean effort on the part of the Soviet government to improve both the size and quality of the merchant marine, the success of which can be judged from the fact that, by the middle of the decade, the fleet moved from 12th to 5th in the world rankings and over four-fifths of its vessels were less than ten years old. In 1958 the Wismar shipyard, one of the first in the Soviet bloc to be rebuilt after the war, had started on the construction of a class of nineteen handsome 4,871 ton *Mikhail Kalinin* class passenger ships intended for cruising as well as a range of military, scientific and supply purposes, so it was really little surprise when the order was placed for a class of similar but far larger liners.

The new vessels, all of which were named after famous poets and authors who had been born within the then powerful and extensive Russian Empire, had a gross tonnage of 19,860 and measured 578ft overall with a beam of 77ft and a draft of 26ft. Officially named the *Ivan Franko* class after the lead ship, they were also widely referred to as the 'Russian Author' or 'Russian Poet' class, and it is the latter which is used throughout this book. With a clear family resemblance to their smaller predecessors, they were the result of extensive tank testing which was claimed to have yielded a high degree of hydro and aerodynamic efficiency. Despite not initially being fitted with stabilisers, their deep draught and sea-kindly hulls, which were also ice-strengthened to 'following an icebreaker in broken ice' class, quickly earned them a reputation for stability and comfort in heavy seas.

The pronounced sheer of their hulls was complimented by a powerful, raked bow and a rounded stern which was drawn into an unusual and particularly elegant point. Above this rose a tiered superstructure, a streamlined funnel and single mast which combined to give the ships a particularly well-balanced and racy profile which was complemented by a simple but striking livery: their black hulls were given a deep red boot-topping and girdled by a single, thin white line which was broken only by the ship's name at the bow. Their upperworks were painted white and their funnels bore the familiar red band and yellow hammer and sickle motif of the Soviet Merchant Marine. Representing the very pinnacle of Soviet design, they turned heads wherever they went and were widely acknowledged as some of the most beautiful passenger ships afloat.

Given the mind-set of the time, the proliferation of state-of-the-art aerials atop the bridge gave rise to inevitable rumours of 'spy ship' activities! This impression was probably strengthened by the fact that the class were fitted with unusually powerful deck gear including six large derricks, two located aft and four more to serve their forward holds and specially strengthened foredecks which were designed to carry heavy loads. The first four ships were built with large holds capable of swallowing up to 1,500 tons of cargo, and side-loading ramps in the forward shell plating through which cars or military vehicles could be

embarked. Combined with a cruising range of over 10,000 miles and a maximum speed of 22 knots, their potential as fast military transports was obvious.

Their interiors, which will be described in detail in the next chapter, made extensive use of modern, wipe-clean materials such as formica and, although both comfortable and functional, appeared somewhat spartan by western standards. Most of the public rooms together with a large glass-enclosed swimming pool, were concentrated on the Saloon Deck, one level below the Boat Deck where a number of high-grade cabins were located. Unusually for the period, the rest of their cabins also enjoyed outside views although not all had private facilities, their occupants having to use the bathroom blocks which occupied the inboard areas of all three principal accommodation decks.

The first of the class, the *Ivan Franko,* ran her sea trials in October 1964 to be followed at regular intervals over the next eight years by her four sister ships. Following their introduction the ships were variously employed in transatlantic liner voyages to Montreal and later New York, and cruises from various countries, including Britain, West Germany and Canada, to Scandinavia, the Baltic, Mediterranean, Canaries, Cuba and elsewhere. A little later, several of the sisters undertook line voyages from the UK to Australia and New Zealand and also offered cruises out of Sydney and Auckland during the southern hemisphere summer seasons. Many of these cruises and voyages were carried out under charter to the Soviet-owned but UK and Australian-based Charter Travel Club (CTC) and its German equivalent, Transocean D. Oltmann & Co (Transocean)of which more will be said in subsequent chapters.

What follows is a brief outline of the career of each sister, in order of building.

Ivan Franko

The first of the 'Russian Poet' class was laid down at the Wismar shipyard as number 125 and launched on 15th June 1963 as the *Ivan Franko,* after the famous Ukrainian writer and poet. She was delivered to her designated owning company, The Black Sea Shipping Company of Odessa, on 14th November 1963. It fell to her to introduce the prestigious new liner service from Leningrad to Montreal and she successfully settled into a mixed programme of transatlantic voyages and cruises.

In 1974 she underwent a refit which saw her Boat and Saloon decks extended forward, creating three 'steps' in her superstructure in place of the previous two. All of the sisters in turn underwent the same modifications which, although detracting very slightly from their beauty, added considerably to the quality of their public rooms and accommodation and increased their gross tonnage to 20,064. It is interesting to note that one of the alterations (also applied to her Black Sea Shipping sisters *Taras Shevchenko* and *Shota Rustaveli)* was the conversion of her Bridge Deck lounge into six penthouse suites, each with a lounge, separate bedroom and balcony. The provision of balconies,

which are commonplace on board today's cruise vessels, was highly innovative and an early indication of things to come. Each ship was also fitted with stabilizers by this time.

During 1968 CTC chartered the *Ivan Franko* for a voyage to Australia and New Zealand but, at the last moment, her sister ship the *Shota Rustaveli* took her place. It was not until December 1979, and finally

Taken in July 1965 this striking view of **Ivan Franko** shows her as built. Note particularly the four large cargo cranes and the arrangement of the decks forward of the bridge. (John Hendy)

Alexandr Pushkin at sea on 1st June 1968. (FotoFlite)

military transport role. Several observers recall that she often showed outward signs of heavy use, and generally appeared to be the least well-maintained of the sisters.

She continued in operation until 1997 when she was laid up and sold to Pollucks Shipping of St Vincent, who renamed her the *Frank* and quickly re-sold her to ship breakers in India. She arrived at Alang on 21st July 1997 where she was beached and broken up.

Alexandr Pushkin

The second of the class was launched on 26th April 1964 and allocated to the Baltic Steamship Company of Leningrad. Destined to become the much-loved *Marco Polo* in 1991, her Soviet career is described in detail in the next chapter.

Taras Shevchenko

The third sister was laid down as yard number 127, launched on 16th January 1965 and named after the famous Ukrainian poet, writer, artist, public and political figure whose literary heritage is regarded as the foundation of modern Ukrainian literature.

She was delivered to the Black Sea Shipping Company on 26th April 1967 and immediately began cruising from Soviet and European ports to the Black Sea, Mediterranean, Scandinavia and the Canaries. In 1973, under charter to CTC, she made a voyage to Australia from where she ran a series of Pacific cruises before returning to the UK in March 1974.

In 1975 she underwent a refit which saw her superstructure extended forward, a large new Music Salon created at the forward end of the Saloon Deck, and various improvements made to lounges and accommodation. With the work completed she mixed European cruising with several more voyages to Australia and New Zealand and, on 30th March 1979, set off on another line voyage from Southampton which, going outwards via Panama and homeward via Suez, would eventually take her round the world. On arrival at Sydney her long-distance passengers were offered a number of options to fill a fortnight ashore, while the ship set off on a 14-night South Pacific Cruise. When the ship returned they re-embarked and departed Sydney on 19th May for the UK.

Late in 1984 the *Taras Shevchenko* (together with her sister *Shota Rustaveli*) received another refit and emerged in an all-white livery, much to the surprise and irritation of CTC whose 1985 brochures featured her in her usual black hull. She continued to visit the Antipodes until, in May 1980, as one of its responses to the Soviet invasion of Afghanistan, the Australian government banned Soviet fishing vessels and cruise ships

under charter to CTC, that the *Ivan Franco* finally made it to the Antipodes, arriving in Sydney on 7th December. From there she offered two South Pacific cruises before departing on 26th January 1980 for an epic 66-day expedition voyage to New Zealand, South America, around Cape Horn and back to Sydney via the Panama Canal and Pacific Ocean. Thereafter she made two more Pacific cruises before returning to Europe to resume her more usual pattern of cruising. *Ivan Franco* undertook charters for Jahn Reisen of Munich and would also appear to have spent significant amounts of time working under the direction of the Soviet Military. She was sighted off the coasts of both Cuba and Angola on a number of occasions, and appears to have been very hard-worked in her

Taras Shevchenko moored 'stern to' at Valetta, Malta, shows off her original, racy profile to perfection. (Ian Boyle, Simplon Postcards)

from operating out of Australian Ports. The ban lasted for three years until a change of government allowed the 'Poet class' liners to return once again. The *Taras Shevchenko* made her last visit to Australia and New Zealand in February 1986 during her final world cruise.

In 1997 she was sold to Ocean Agencies of Odessa, Ukraine. After yet another refit she commenced a new cruise programme but her owners soon found themselves in financial difficulties. Whilst preparing to depart on a three-week cruise from Piraeus in June 1998, the ship was impounded for debt. Negotiations eventually resulted in her being allowed to sail to a shipyard at Ilyichevsk, Ukraine, where she remained laid up for the next five years. In 2003 she re-entered service for Antarktika JSC, but the new operator proved even less successful than its predecessor and within a year the ship was laid up once again. This time there was no reprieve and she was quickly sold to Bangladeshi ship breakers. Renamed *Tara* for her delivery voyage, and still looking immaculate, she arrived at Chittagong in late January 2005 where she was run onto the beach and quickly dismantled.

Shota Rustaveli

The fourth 'Russian Poet', yard number 128, was launched on 29th December 1966 and named *Shota Rustaveli* after the 12th century Georgian poet. She was delivered to the Black Sea Shipping Company of Odessa on 30th June 1968 and, in addition to all the usual cruises from European ports, was the first of the sisters to visit Australia and New Zealand. Under charter to CTC she sailed from Southampton on 14th October 1968, passing through the Panama Canal to visit Auckland and arrive at Sydney on 15th November. On this first occasion she remained in port for only one day before commencing her homeward passage, but in subsequent years she remained long enough to offer a number of South Pacific cruises before returning to England. Passages between Auckland and Sydney and vice versa were also available if space permitted.

On each of her early voyages from the UK *Shota Rustaveli* would have derived useful income by carrying a number of passengers who were emigrating to Australia under the 'Assisted Migration Scheme'. On the condition that they remained in Australia for at least two years, adults were offered a government-subsidised fare of only £10 for the voyage, while accompanying children travelled free. Several million UK citizens took advantage of the scheme between 1945 and 1982 and the flow reached its peak in 1962 when 80,000 so called 'Ten Pound Poms' were welcomed into Australia.

As the ship which established CTC's line voyages to Australia, the

Taras Shevchenko at sea, showing her post-1984 all-white livery and the alterations made to her forward superstructure during 1975. (Fotoflite)

Still looking immaculate in her Antarktika JSC livery the former *Taras Shevchenko*, her name shortened to *Tara* for the delivery voyage, passes through the Bosphorus en route to ship breaker's yard at Chittagong. (Mehemet Yapici -www.fotoio.com)

Shota Rustaveli after the extension of her forward superstructure. (Fotoflite)

The end of the line: ***Assedo***, ex ***Shota Rustaveli*** being broken up on the beach at Alang, India, during December 2003. (Peter Knego)

Shota Rustaveli became well-known to English speaking travellers on opposite sides of the globe and continued her pattern of operation until 1973 when it became her turn to undergo the same refit that her older sisters had already received. She was replaced by *Taras Shevchenko* for one season only but then resumed her annual migration to the southern hemisphere. Such was the demand for both the line voyage and the Pacific cruises that, for the winter of 1975-6 CTC decided to send two ships south; *Taras Shevchenko* taking the usual route through the Panama Canal, while a fully-booked *Shota Rustaveli* offered an innovative voyage of discovery along the coast of South America before rounding Cape Horn and heading directly for Auckland and Sydney. In 1977 and 1978 she sailed outwards via the Suez Canal and homeward via Panama, making what turned out to be her final departure from Australia on 20th May 1978. Upon her return to Europe she undertook two more cruises before, along with most of her sisters and many other passenger ships, she was taken up by MORPASFLOT to carry large numbers of young people and their support teams to and from the 11th World Festival of Youth and Students in Cuba. This enormous event with its motto 'For anti-imperialist solidarity, peace and friendship' attracted 18,500 participants from 145 countries and required huge carrying capacity, so it was little wonder that all of the 'Poets' ' normal cruises were suspended for the duration of the games.

Back in Europe she continued her popular CTC cruise programme with her final sailing on the British market listed for September 1978. She received another refit, extended decks aft and a white hull and was able to give almost two decades more faithful service to her charterers such as Transtours in France, GrandiViaggi in Italy, NUR Neckermann in Germany and to her Soviet and Ukrainian owners before being sold in late 1997 to Ocean Agencies Ltd of Odessa. She was laid up at Ilyichevsk where she was soon joined by her sister *Taras Shevchenko*. There she was well-maintained by a skeleton crew until sold in 2000 to Kaalbye Shipping International of Kingstown, St. Vincent. She was given a thorough refit, re-named the *Assedo* (her port of registry, Odessa in reverse!) and re-entered the Russian cruise market with reasonable success, until sold to Indian ship breakers at Alang where she arrived on 28th November 2003.

Mikhail Lermontov

The fifth and, as it turned out, final member of the class (Yard Number 129) slid down the ways of the Wismar shipyard on 31st December 1970 to be given the name of the famous Russian romantic poet, writer and painter, often referred to as 'the poet of the Caucasus'. She was delivered to the Baltic Shipping Company of Leningrad on 18th March 1972 and commenced her maiden cruise from Bremerhaven to the Canary Islands on 21st April.

She embarked on her first transatlantic voyage to Montreal on 9th June 1972 and a year later was switched to serve New York where she arrived for the first time on 11th June 1973 from Leningrad, Bremerhaven, Tilbury and Le Havre. She continued on the New York service until 1980 although the bulk of her time was spent cruising. She departed from Southampton on her first voyage to Australia and New Zealand in January 1977, sailing outwards via Panama and homewards

via Melbourne, Fremantle and Suez, thus completing her first circumnavigation. Although she was immensely popular, it quickly became evident that her cabins, most of which did not have private facilities, did not compare favourably with newer western cruise ships which were then appearing in the market. In 1982, therefore, CTC provided £12 million to give her a far more extensive refit than any of her sisters enjoyed, in order to fit her for world-class cruising. Decks were extended, many of her public rooms enlarged or re-modelled and all of them were redecorated. She was also fitted with two large, modern tenders, at a cost of £75,000 each, for shuttling cruise passengers ashore

Shota Rustaveli (right) enters Grand Harbour Malta where her sister ship *Taras Shevchenko* is already berthed at the quay. Both ships are displaying the blue funnel bands and black trident emblems of the Black Sea Shipping company which they wore under later Ukrainian ownership. (Ian Boyle, Simplon Postcards)

from anchorages. All of her cabins were made en suite and the ship emerged, resplendent in an all-white livery, to set off on her 1983 round-the-world voyage outward via Panama and the Pacific, and homeward via the Indian Ocean and Suez. Her impressive 95 night itinerary took her from Tilbury to Madeira, Antigua, Havana, Cozumel, Cristobal (Panama Canal transit), Balboa, Guayaquil, Callao, Pitcairn Island, Tahiti, Fiji, Yokohama, Hong Kong, Bangkok, Singapore, Colombo, Male, Aden, Suez (canal transit), Port Said, Piraeus, Naples and Gibraltar, but did not touch at Australia where a ban on Soviet vessels was still in place.

Once the ban was lifted the *Mikhail Lermontov* was able to undertake successful return voyages to Sydney in both 1984 and 1985, offering a selection of Pacific cruises while she was in the Southern Hemisphere. On 7th February 1986 she departed from Sydney on a two-week cruise which was due to take her to the Bay of Islands, Auckland, Tauranga,

Wellington, Picton, Queen Charlotte, Doubtful and Milford Sounds. With 372 passengers and 348 crew on board she left Picton at 1500hrs on 16th February bound for Milford Sound, under the command of Capt. Vladislav Vorobyev and with an experienced pilot on board. The latter, Capt. Don Jamieson, was also Picton harbourmaster and his presence should have ensured the absolute safety of the liner. However, things were to turn out very differently.

Things got off to a bad start when the ship's stern touched bottom and she nearly grounded by the bow while leaving Picton, and Jamieson then proceeded to take an unusual and risky course which took him dangerously close to various islands and headlands. Despite Capt. Vorobyev's insistence that the ship should be kept in deeper water further off shore and the remonstrations of the officer of the watch, Jamieson then decided to take her through a narrow passage between Cape Jackson

Mikhail Lermontov at sea on 6th June 1972. (FotoFlite)

and the off-lying lighthouse on Jackson Head where, at 1737hrs, she hit rocks and tore a 40ft (12m) gash in her port side, just below the waterline. Three watertight bulkheads were breached and there was an immediate inrush of water .

Capt. Vorobyev, having rushed to the bridge and assessed the situation decided to try to beach his ship in shallow water. The crippled *Mikhail Lermontov*, with her 12° list increasing by the minute, limped slowly south westwards towards Port Gore where she ran gently aground and thanks to Capt. Vorobyev's calmness and quick thinking everyone on board except for one engineer was evacuated safely in life rafts and boats and taken ashore in various rescue ships. Sadly, however, a complete loss of electrical power at 1918hrs meant that neither the main engines, pumps or anchor winches could be operated and, on a rising tide and now listing by 40° to starboard, she drifted back into deeper water, rolled over and sank in 115ft (35m) of water. A New Zealand Ministry of Transport preliminary inquiry into the loss placed the blame firmly on Capt. Jamieson's shoulders, concluding that his actions were explained, in part at least, by a combination of extreme tiredness and a desire to give the passengers the closest possible view of the passing coastline. Its findings, however, remain controversial and have provided the subject for several books and much on-going debate. *Mikhail Lermontov*, meanwhile, remains where she foundered providing a vast and popular target for wreck divers.

Thus, with the passage of time, four of the lovely sister ships disappeared from the world's oceans, leaving only *Alexandr Pushkin*, renamed *Marco Polo* from 1991, to remind us one of the most stylish classes of passenger ships constructed during the 20th century. Her history is the subject of the remainder of this book.

Mikhail Lermontov alongside Tilbury Landing Stage, London, displaying her post-1982 all-white livery. (FotoFlite)

Alexandr Pushkin depicted on an early Baltic Steamship Company advertising leaflet. (Richard Bastow)

Т/Х **АЛЕКСАНДР ПУШКИН**

M/S ALEXANDR PUSHKIN
M/S ALEXANDER PUSCHKIN

БАЛТИЙСКОЕ МОРСКОЕ ПАРОХОДСТВО
BALTIC STEAMSHIP COMPANY
BALTISCHE SEEREEDEREI

ALEXANDR PUSHKIN, THE SOVIET YEARS

The ship which was destined to become the much-loved *Marco Polo* was laid down at the shipyard of V.E.B. Mathias Thesen Werft at Wismar, a Baltic Sea port about 80 miles from Hamburg in what was then East Germany, as Yard Number 126. No record exists of the name of her designer, but it is widely assumed that she was designed 'in house' by the shipyard itself.

Launched on 26th April 1964, she was named the *Alexandr Pushkin* in honour of the man who many regard as Russia's greatest poet. Born into a wealthy Moscow family on 6th June 1799, Pushkin wrote his first poem at the age of fifteen and his talent was soon recognised within the Russian literary establishment. His subsequent works included numerous narrative poems, plays including 'Boris Godunov', prose, fairy tales in verse, and the famous verse novel 'Eugene Onegin', while many of his works were set to music as songs and operas. Pushkin was also politically active and, because of his interest in social reform, became something of a thorn in the side of the authorities who moved him away from the capital and at one stage placed him in internal exile on his mother's country estate. Always a volatile character, he died in 1837 from wounds received during a duel with his wife's alleged lover, leaving behind a literary and musical legacy of tremendous importance.

Like her older sister *Ivan Franko,* the new liner had a gross tonnage of 19,860 and measured 578ft (176.1m) overall, with a beam of 77ft (8.1m) and a draft of 26.6ft (8.1m). With her powerful raked bow, elegant stern and shapely, ice-strengthened hull, she was strikingly beautiful and modern in appearance. At the forward end her white superstructure rose from a strengthened foredeck in two perfectly proportioned steps, before ascending to the dramatically curved bridge front above. Surmounted by a single mast and streamlined funnel, the superstructure then descended in more gradual steps towards the stern. The overall effect was a delight to the eye. She was immediately designated the flagship of the Baltic Steamship Company, a position she continued to occupy until displaced by her younger sister, the *Mikhail Lermontov,* in 1972.

Powered by two 7-cylinder, 21,000BHP SulzerRD76 diesel engines driving twin screws, she had a maximum speed of 22 knots but was designed to operate at 20.5 knots on the Atlantic crossing and more

A view over the rooftops of Wismar in 1966. The shipyard where **Alexandr Pushkin** and her sisters were built can be seen in the top left hand corner. (CMV)

Alexandr Pushkin as she appeared when new. Note her heavy deck gear and her crew drawn up on the foredeck, naval fashion, for entering harbour. (Richard Bastow)

economical speeds while cruising. She could carry 130 first class and 620 tourist class passengers on the transatlantic route or 750 in one class while cruising.

She was delivered to her owners, the Baltic Steamship Company of Leningrad on 14th August 1965, but the precise date of her maiden voyage has yet to be confirmed. Unfortunately, the records held at her owner's Leningrad office were destroyed by fire and others have disappeared, while other written sources are fragmented and contradictory which makes piecing together the ship's early career frustratingly difficult.

It is believed that there was a short gap between the ship's delivery and her maiden cruise, which was probably under charter to a Scandinavian organisation. Thereafter, she began what was to become a wide range of cruises which took her to Scandinavia, Western Europe, the Mediterranean and the Canary Islands. Between 1966 and 1979 these were operated on an agency basis for the British or German markets although the ship also became popular with Dutch travellers who would embark when she called at Rotterdam .

The ship's Master throughout these early years was Captain Aram Mikhailovich Oganov, Ph.D. Born in 1925 at Zakataly, near Baku in Azerbaidzhan, he graduated from Baku Marine College with honours, completed his education at the Navigation Faculty of Leningrad Higher Marine Engineering College and in 1945 joined Baltic Steamship Company as a navigator. He gained his Master's ticket in 1952 and his first commands were cargo vessels before he transferred to the passenger fleet as Captain of *Estonia*, a 300 passenger capacity liner built in 1960 that primarily worked the Leningrad – London service. He was appointed to the brand new *Alexandr Pushkin* in 1964 and retained command until 1972 when he was given the command of the newest of the 'Russian Poets', the *Mikhail Lermontov*, in which he inaugurated the Leningrad – New York service and revived a route which had last been operated in 1949. He was replaced on board the *Alexandr Pushkin* by Capt. Gradsky and later by Capt. Vitaly Segal. Aram Oganov rose to become the Commandant of the Baltic Shipping Company's passenger fleet, trained twenty nine ship captains, was honoured with the title 'Hero of Socialist Labour' and awarded two 'Orders of Lenin' together with numerous

An early Baltic Steamship Company coloured postcard showing *Alexandr Pushkin* at sea. (Ian Boyle, Simplon Postcards)

MS IVAN FRANKO

SKYFOTOS LTD.

NEW

First vessels of a series of large passenger liners to be built for the Baltic and Black Sea Steamship Lines completed in 1964/1965. These vessels offer high standard of accommodation and social amenities for passengers. Excellent Russian and European cuisine. Complete relaxation combined with the friendliness and courtesy of the crew ensures a pleasant, interesting and restful voyage.

19860 gross tons
service speed 20 knots
accommodation for 750 passengers
fully air conditioned

МMФ СССР

MS ALEX. PUSHKIN

A 1965/66 advertising leaflet. (Peter Newell)

M.S. ALEXANDER PUSHKIN was completed in 1965, of 19,860 gross tons with accommodation for 750 passengers for 23 cars, service speed 20 knots. The vessel offers a high standard of accommodation with the usual variety of social rooms including cinema, library, games rooms, also two swimming pools with heated water. The ship is fully air conditioned.

The passenger accommodation consists of one-, two- and four-berth outside cabins. On the Boat Deck, the one and two-berth cabins have private facilities as have also those on the Promenade Deck aft.

There is an observation verandah with adjacent bar on the Bridge Deck. The Saloon Deck is devoted exclusively to passenger social amenities offering a Music Saloon, two cafes, kiosks for sale of souvenirs, magazines, etc., smoking room, games room and bar which are interconnected, play room, cinema, library and reading room, ladies' and gents' hairdressers, large swimming pool with adjoining bar. The promenade deck has a small warm weather pool for children adjoining their play room. The dining room on the Main Deck amid-ships occupies the whole width of the vessel.

Canadian Service Schedule 1966

LENINGRAD	Dep.	13 April 24.00	15 May 24.00	16 June 24.00	22 July 24.00	23 Aug. 24.00	25 Sept. 24.00
HELSINKI	Arr.	11.00 14 April	11.00 16 May	11.00 17 June	11.00 23 July	11.00 24 Aug.	11.00 26 Sept.
	Dep.	18.00	18.00	18.00	18.00	18.00	18.00
COPENHAGEN	Arr.	14.00 16 April	14.00 18 May	14.00 19 June	14.00 25 July	14.00 26 Aug.	14.00 28 Sept.
	Dep.	21.00	21.00	21.00	21.00	21.00	21.00
LONDON	Arr.	12.00 18 April	12.00 20 May	12.00 21 June	12.00 27 July	12.00 28 Aug.	12.00 30 Sept.
	Dep.	22.00	22.00	22.00	22.00	22.00	22.00
QUEBEC	Arr.	07.00 26 April	07.00 28 May	07.00 29 June	07.00 4 Aug.	07.00 5 Sept.	07.00 8 Oct.
	Dep.	17.00	17.00	17.00	17.00	17.00	17.00
MONTREAL	Arr.	07.00 27 April	07.00 29 May	07.00 30 June	07.00 5 Aug.	07.00 6 Sept.	07.00 9 Oct.
	Dep.	30 April 11.00	1 June 11.00	4 July 11.00	8 Aug. 11.00	10 Sept. 11.00	12 Oct. 11.00
LONDON	Arr.	07.00 8 May	07.00 9 June	07.00 12 July	07.00 16 Aug.	07.00 18 Sept.	07.00 20 Oct.
	Dep.	14.00	14.00	14.00	14.00	14.00	14.00
COPENHAGEN	Arr.	07.00 10 May	07.00 11 June	07.00 14 July	07.00 18 Aug.	07.00 20 Sept.	07.00 22 Oct.
	Dep.	15.00	15.00	15.00	15.00	15.00	15.00
HELSINKI	Arr.	13.00 12 May	13.00 13 June	13.00 16 July	13.00 20 Aug.	13.00 22 Sept.	13.00 24 Oct.
	Dep.	20.00	20.00	20.00	21 Aug. 06.30	23 Sept. 06.30	25 Oct. 06.30
LENINGRAD	Arr.	09.00 13 May	09.00 14 June	09.00 17 July	20.00 21 Aug.	20.00 23 Sept.	20.00 25 Oct.

HELSINKI	COPENHAGEN	MONTREAL	MOSCOW	LENINGRAD
Travel Agency Kaleva	Danish State Railways	March Shipping Agency	Intourist	Intourist
13 SNELLMANINKATU	42 FREDERIKSBORGGADE	400 CRAIG STREET WEST	22, 24 SVERDLOV SQUARE	39 HERTZEN STREET
Cables: Mackasnel Helsinki	Cables: Noereroute Copenhagen	Cables: Mrship Montreal	Cables: Intourist Moscow	Cables: Intourist Leningrad

CANADA
BY
'ALEXANDR PUSHKIN'

LONDON TO MONTREAL 1971

E. H. MUNDY & CO. (PASSENGERS) LTD.
154 HIGH STREET
SOUTHAMPTON SO1 0BT
TEL. 23941
ABTA No. 4506

BALTIC STEAMSHIP CO. U.S.S.R.

CANADA
BALTIC STEAMSHIP LINE

DISCOVERY TRAVELS LTD.,
805, LONDON ROAD,
WESTCLIFF-ON-SEA, ESSEX

M.S. ALEXANDER PUSHKIN

Montreal · Quebec
FROM
London
Copenhagen
Helsinki
Leningrad

including LONDON - LENINGRAD Service

SAILING SCHEDULES
and FARE TARIFFS
1966

Alexandr Pushkin's 1966 transatlantic schedule. (Peter Newell)

Soviet 12 and 16 rouble commemorative stamps produced shortly after *Alexandr Pushkin*'s entry into service. (Richard Clammer)

Two advertising leaflets for the transatlantic service to Canada. Note the selection of ports listed in 1966. (Peter Newell)

17

The BALTIC STEAMSHIP COMPANY

PASSENGER LIST

T/X „АЛЕКСАНДР ПУШКИН"
M.S. ALEXANDR PUSHKIN

19,860 Tons Gross Register (U.S.S.R. Registry)

...wly built modern Soviet passenger liner "ALEXANDR PUSHKIN" which
...the name of the great Russian poet will be your lucky strike. Speed,
...beauty, air conditioned comfort throughout, every newest convenience
...cility – all are combined in the design and construction of this luxurious
...From the moment you board the "ALEXANDR PUSHKIN" you feel comfort,
...y and friendliness surrounding you.

...sel is 176 metres long and 24 metres wide. Two powerful engines are
... with a total capacity of 21,000 horsepower, with an average speed of
...ts. Long distances can be covered in any weather with perfect ease.
...odation for 670 passengers including first and tourist class. Space is also
...e for 30 automobiles and 1500 tons of cargo.

Master	Captain Aram M. Oganov
Staff Captain	Edward Epstein
Chief Officer	Genady Terekhow
Chief Engineer	Vasily Tkatchev
Chief Purser	Elia Dolgintsev
Chief Physician	Nikolai Baushew
Chief Steward	Valentin Mochennikov

...FROM MONTREAL, FRIDAY, APRIL 28, 1967

...NGRAD VIA LONDON, BREMERHAVEN AND HELSINKI

THE BALTIC STEAMSHIP COMPANY
General Agents
MARCH SHIPPING AGENCY

T/X „АЛЕКСАНДР ПУШКИН"
M.S. ALEXANDR PUSHKIN

1967 SAILINGS

EASTBOUND TO EUROPE

Due London (Tilbury)	Due Bremerhaven	Due Helsinki	Due Leningrad
1967	1967	1967	1967
May 6	May 7	May 10	May 11
June 9	June 10	June 13	June 14
July 12	July 13	July 16	July 17
Aug. 26	Aug. 27	Aug. 30	Aug. 31
Sept. 27	Sept. 28	Oct. 1	Oct. 2
Oct. 31	Nov. 1	Nov. 4	Nov. 5

WESTBOUND FROM EUROPE

Leave Helsinki		Leave Bremerhaven	Leave London (Tilbury)	Due Quebec	Due Montreal
...67		1967	1967	1967	1967
May 16	May 17	April 17	April 18	April 26	April 27
June 16	June 17	May 20	May 21	May 29	May 30
July 31	Aug. 1	June 20	June 21	June 29	June 30
Sept. 3	Sept. 4	Aug. 7	Aug. 5	Aug. 13	Aug. 14
Oct. 8	Oct. 8	Sept. 7	Sept. 8	Sept. 16	Sept. 17
		Oct. 11	Oct. 12	Oct. 20	Oct. 21

This page: A passenger list dated 28th April 1967 whose early pages contained a list
of the ship's officers and the 1967 transatlantic timetable. (Richard Bastow)

Opposite: A selection of pages from Alexandr Pushkin's 1968 Sailings & Fares leaflet.
(Bjorn Larsson)

THE BALTIC STEAMSHIP COMPANY
HEAD OFFICE
5 Mezhevoi Canal, Leningrad, L-35, U.S.S.R.
Telephones: 16-90-57, 16-93-23
Cables Morflot/Leningrad. Telex: 1501, 1502

MARCH SHIPPING AGENCIES L...
General Agents for North America

MONTREAL, QUE.
400 Craig Street West
Cables: Marship, Montreal. Telex: 01-2410. Tel. 84...

TORONTO, ONT.
83 King Street East
Cables: Marship, Toronto. Tel. 366-2586

NEW YORK, N.Y. (10017)
March Shipping Passenger Services
51 East 42nd Street, Suite 1209. Tel. 697-1990

* **QUEBEC, QUE.**
Ramsey Greig & Co. Ltd., 1026 St. John Street.
Cables: Greig, Quebec. Tel. 529-9548

OFFICES AND PRINCIPAL PASSENGER

MOSCOW
— Central Agency for International Passenger Transp...
11/1, Marx Avenue. Cables: Moragentstvo Mos...
Telex: Moscow 134

MOSCOW
— Travel Bureau Intourist, 1, Marx Avenue.
Cables: Intourist Moscow

LENINGRAD
— Intourist, 39, Hertzen Street.
Cables: Intourist Leningrad

BREMEN
— Transocean (General Agents for the Federal Rep...
Martinistrasse 10-11
Cables: Transocean. Telex: 024-4362. Tel. 3...
Also offices in Berlin, Essen, Frankfurt/M., Hamburg, K...

HELSINKI
— Kaleva Travel Agency
13 Snellmaninkatu. Cables: Matkansel Hels...
— Travel Bureau OY Lomamatka
31 Yrjönkatu. Cables: Lomamatka Helsinki...

LONDON, E.C.3
— Stelp & Leighton Ltd.
9-13, Fenchurch Buildings, Fenchurch Str...
Cables: Sandilpass London. Telex: 28356...

Port Agent

SEE YOUR LOCAL TRAV...

PRINTED IN CANADA

ms ALEXANDR PUSHKIN

1968
sailings & fares

The BALTIC STEAMSHIP COMPANY

SAFETY INFORMATION
The M.S. Alexandr Pushkin registered in the U.S.S.R. and built in 1965 meets the International Safety Standard for new ships developed in 1960.

NORTH AMERICAN SERVICE
(Subject to Change Without Notice)

SEASONAL DATES—1968
(All dates inclusive)

HIGH SEASON
Eastbound: June 1 to July 31
Westbound: July 16 to Sept. 15

INTERMEDIATE SEASON
Eastbound: April 1 to May 31 - Aug. 1 to Sept. 15
Westbound: May 16 to July 15-Sept. 16 to Oct. 31

THRIFT SEASON
Eastbound: Jan. 1 to March 31 & Sept. 16 to Dec. 31
Westbound: Jan. 1 to May 15 & Nov. 1 to Dec. 31

EASTBOUND

HIGH SEASON DATES SHOWN IN BLACK   INTERMEDIATE SEASON DATES SHOWN IN BLUE   THRIFT SEASON DATES SHOWN IN RED

MONTREAL	BREMERHAVEN	HELSINKI	LENINGRAD
	Expected: Arrival 3 p.m. Departure 8 p.m. (Local Time)	Expected: Arrival 1 p.m. Departure 8 p.m. (Local Time)	Expected Arrival 9 a.m. except ▲ 8 p.m. (Local Time)
	Wed. May 8	Sat. May 11	Sun. May 12
	Sat. June 8	Tue. June 11	Wed. June 12
	Mon. July 8	Thu. July 11	Fri. July 12
	Sat. Aug. 24	*Tue. Aug. 27	▲Wed. Aug. 28
	Wed. Sept. 25	*Sat. Sept. 28	▲Sun. Sept. 29
	Sat. Oct. 26	*Tue. Oct. 29	▲Wed. Oct. 30

*Departure daybreak following day

LONDON	QUEBEC	MONTREAL
April 18	Fri. April 26	Sat. April 27

M. S. ALEXANDR PUSHKIN

BERMUDA SUMMER CRUISE — 13 DAYS

Sailing from Montreal, July 27, 1968

STATEROOMS ARE OUTSIDE
AND FULLY AIR-CONDITIONED

FARES IN CANADIAN DOLLARS

(per person)

Staterooms with private bath, shower and ... on Boat Deck:
103, 104 — single staterooms $775.00
101, 102 — double bedded staterooms $745.00

Bedded Staterooms with private shower ... toilet on Boat Deck:
106 to 114, 121 to 126 . . . . $705.00

Bedded Staterooms, with private shower ... toilet on Promenade Deck:
247 to 277 and 279 . . . . $675.00

Double or Single Staterooms with Bed and Upper Pullman Berth, private shower and toilet on ... Deck:
115 to 120, 127 to 142 . . . . $560.00

Staterooms with Two Lower Beds and Divan on ..., Promenade and Second Decks:
201, 202, 205, 206, 219, 220, 245, 246, 331 to 336, ... 342, 344, 350, 406, 407, 410, 414, 415, 418, ... 429, 433, 437 to 439, 441 to 444 . . . . . . $475.00

Staterooms with Two Lower Beds and Divan on Third Deck:
501, 502, 505 to 508, 513, 514, 516, 521 to 524, ... 529, 530, 532, 537 to 540, 545 to 548, 565, 567, ... 569, 571, 573, 575, 579 . . . . $400.00

... Berth Staterooms with Upper Pullman Berth ... Lower Bed and Divan on Promenade, Main ... Third Deck:
203, 204, 207 to 218, 221 to 244, 301 to 330, 337 to ... 340, 343, 345, 346, 348, 401 to 405, 408, 409, 411 ... to 413, 416, 417, 419 to 428, 430 to 432, 434 to ... 436, 440 . . . . $345.00

... Two Berth Staterooms with Upper Pullman Berth ... Lower Bed and Divan on Third Deck:
503, 504, 509 to 512, 515, 517 to 520, 525 to 528, ... 531, 533 to 536, 541 to 544, 577 . . . . . . $295.00

Single room occupancy—One full fare plus 50%. Sharing of accommodation acceptable.

Family plan — Children under 12 years of age sharing same stateroom with two adults $100. Over 12 $200.

Bermuda Port Tax —$3.05 per person

CRUISE ITINERARY

The MS ALEXANDR PUSHKIN will sail from Iberville Ocean Terminal Shed 5 (reached via Entrance Foot of McGill Street).

MONTREAL Embarkation Sat. July 27 between 8:30 and 11:30 p.m.
Leave Montreal at Midnight.

QUEBEC

SAGUENAY RIVER

BERMU...

ST. PIE... MIQUE...

GASPE...

QUEBE...

MONT...

Double ... Staterooms with Bed and Upper Pullman Berth, private shower and toilet on Boat Deck:
115 to 120, 127 to 142. | 427 390 369

TOURIST CLASS (Per Bed)

Twin Bedded Staterooms, with private shower and toilet on Promenade Deck:
247 to 277 and 279. | 335 313 298 292 367 340 319 303 319 325 400 378 360

Two Berth Staterooms with Upper Pullman Berth and Lower Bed on Promenade, Main and Second Decks:
203, 204, 207 to 218, 221 to 244, 301 to 330, 337 to 340, 343, 345, 346, 348, 401 to 405, 408, 409, 411 to 413, 416, 417, 419 to 428, 430 to 432, 434 to 436, 440. | 297 275 261 254 241 319 297 282 275 261 356 335 319

Two Berth Staterooms with Upper Pullman Berth and Lower Bed on Third Deck:
503, 504, 509 to 512, 515, 517 to 520, 525 to 528, 531, 533 to 536, 541 to 544, 577. | 292 270 257 248 237 319 292 278 270 257 351 329 313 309 293

Four Berth Staterooms with Two Lower Beds and Two Pullman Upper Berths on Main, Promenade and Second Decks:
201, 202, 205, 206, 219, 220, 245, 246, 331 to 336, 341, 342, 344, 350, 406, 407, 410, 414, 415, 418, 429, 433, 437 to 439, 441 to 444. | 281 259 246 238 226 309 281 267 259 246 340 319 302 309 282

Four Berth Staterooms with Two Lower Beds and Two Upper Pullman Berths on Third Deck:
501, 502, 505 to 508, 513, 514, 516, 521 to 524, 529, 530, 532, 537 to 540, 545 to 548, 565, 567, 569, 571, 573, 575, 579. | 276 255 242 232 220 300 278 264 256 243 337 314 298 293 278

▲ Rooms equipped with Cribs.

CANADIAN PORT CHARGE must be collected on all bookings to and/or from Montreal or Quebec City as follows: First Class or Tourist Class, Adults $1.00 each way; Children 1 to 11 years $0.50 C.F. each way.

LONDON PORT CHARGE must be collected on all bookings to and from London, $1.50 C.F. per Adult each way; Children 1 to 11 years, $0.75 C.F.; Infants nil.

LENINGRAD PORT CHARGE must be collected on all bookings to and from Leningrad at $2.50 C.F. per Adult; Children 1 to 11 years $1.25 C.F.; Infants nil.

CHILDREN'S FARES—The age of infant or child on date of sailing governs the age at the date of outward sailing governs fare for both outward and homeward portions. For round-trip bookings the age at the date of outward sailing

Under 1 year, when accompanied by adult — First Class, $44.00 C.F., Tourist, $22.00 C.F.
1 year and under 12, when occupying room with adult or adults — one-half the adult fare for accommodation occupied.
12 years and over — full fare for accommodation occupied.

 Enclosed Swimming Pool - Top Deck

 Dining Room

 Gymnasium

Penguin Bar

Deluxe Single Stateroom

DECK SPORTS

Supervised Children's Playroom

Alexandr Pushkin and *Mikhail Lermontov* passing at Bremerhaven. (Meriel Lowe)

A Baltic Steamship Company ticket wallet. (Peter Newell)

Samovars. The ship received a very warm reception at Quebec and set sail on her return crossing from Montreal on 27th April.

The line voyages on the Montreal service started off as a two-class operation – First and Tourist – which was a requirement of the Trans-Atlantic Passenger Steamship Conference of which the Baltic Steamship Company was initially a member. The Conference also fixed rates and conditions for the carriage of vehicles, pets, and many other aspects of the operation. The main competitors on the route were the Canadian Pacific vessels *Empress of Canada* and *Empress of England* operating out of Liverpool and Greenock to Quebec and Montreal and the Polish Ocean Line's 1936-built *Batory* which sailed on a Gdynia-Copenhagen-Southampton-Montreal route all of which were equally bound by the rules of the Conference.

Transatlantic voyages were scheduled to spend just under fourteen days at sea, with a three-day turn-round at Montreal and two days alongside in Leningrad. It was possible to buy tickets for a single or return crossing, or for shorter hops between European ports, and the service was particularly appreciated in Finland as the country's first such liner service. Despite initial loadings being rather poor the success of the transatlantic service, which had been dormant since the beginning of the Cold War in the late 1940s, was of great importance to the Soviet government. The regular appearance of such beautiful and state-of-the-art ships in Western ports was certainly a matter of great prestige and may well have served other, less transparent purposes as well! During her third Canadian call when the ship was thrown open to visitors, it was claimed that 10,000 were shown round in two hours and a further 15,000 had to be turned away. Female members of the port staff known as 'Pushkin Girls' acted as ambassadors for the ship whenever she was in Quebec.

During the 1966 season demand increased steadily and six return crossings were advertised, ceasing in October when winter ice began to form in the Baltic and St. Lawrence Seaway. On 29th April that year while she was alongside in Canada a major trade agreement was signed on board for the USSR to take part in Expo 67, (the 1967 International and Universal Exposition) in Montreal. Following being caught in a severe storm towards the end of 1966, *Alexandr Pushkin* was fitted with a pair of Denny-Brown retractable fin stabilizers in March 1967 and thereafter her advertising brochures announced that she was 'fully air-conditioned and stabilized' and offered 'a high standard of accommodation and social amenities for passengers, excellent Russian and European cuisine, complete relaxation combined with the friendliness and courtesy of the crew' all leading to 'a pleasant, interesting and restful voyage'.

lesser medals. He died in St Petersburg (formerly Leningrad) on the 26th September 2008 and is buried in the cemetery of St Seraphim.

It was not until midnight on 13th April 1966 that *Alexandr Pushkin* departed on her first transatlantic liner voyage from Leningrad to Montreal, a service which she initially shared with the *Ivan Franko*. The weather was unusually cold for the time of year and two icebreakers were required to open a channel from Leningrad to Helsinki where she arrived 10 hours late on 15th April. From there her route took her to Copenhagen, London (Tilbury) and thence on an eight-day crossing of the Atlantic to Quebec and finally Montreal. Although only 36 passengers were carried on her maiden crossing they (along with the 87 journalists who embarked for different sections of the voyage) were kept busy on passage by a wide range of entertainments including 'Miss Pushkin' and fancy dress contests with prizes of Russian dolls and

Over the years, the intermediate ports of call on the transatlantic service were to vary considerably. Very sensibly, the Russians seem to have been testing the market to discover where the maximum demand was to be found and on 17th April 1967 *Alexandr Pushkin* made her first call at Bremerhaven, a special commemorative coin being struck to mark the occasion. Departing on 28th April from Montreal on her return voyage, the ship had on board 49 first class passengers and 388 tourist class. Of this total of 437, 104 disembarked at Tilbury, 53 at Bremerhaven, 61 at Helsinki and 219 at Leningrad. It is interesting to note the significant number of younger people, presumably attracted by the competitive fares and the less formal atmosphere on board, who were travelling. These included a sizeable group of American students sailing

Alexandr Pushkin arriving at Montreal in February 1969. Berthed in the background is the Polish Ocean Lines' *Batory* of 1935 which was about to be withdrawn from the transatlantic service and replaced by the new *Stefan Batory*. (Richard Clammer)

to Leningrad as part of a Russian Language Study Tour.

By 1972 a French call had been added and the ship's route was now from Leningrad to Bremerhaven, London (Tilbury), Le Havre and Montreal, while her sister ship *Mikhail Lermontov* terminated at New York instead. Some sources also claim that, during the months either side of her main transatlantic season, the *Alexandr Pushkin* also carried out voyages direct from Leningrad to Cuba, though this is unconfirmed.

It must be remembered that the 1960s was a decade when the world of ocean passenger shipping was undergoing profound change. Boeing 707 airliners, along with Douglas DC-8s had been operating transatlantic and other long-range flights for several years and in April 1966, the very same month in which the *Alexandr Pushkin* completed her maiden voyage to Montreal, the first order was made by Pan American Airlines for twenty five Boeing 747-100 aircraft. This first version of the famous Jumbo Jet had a seating capacity of 452 in a two class configuration and could therefore have accommodated the entire *Pushkin* passenger complement from the voyage described above and crossed the Atlantic in a matter of hours rather than days.

This rapid development of jet airliners saw passengers deserting the traditional ocean liner routes in their droves, and forced established companies such as Cunard to consider their very survival. One by one the great ocean liners such as the *America* (1964), *Queen Mary* (1967), *Queen Elizabeth* (1968) and *United States* (1969) were withdrawn completely, while some smaller vessels such as Cunard's *Mauretania* (scrapped 1965) and *Caronia* (laid up 1969) were given refits and briefly sent cruising. Many of these vessels, sumptuous and magnificent as they were, had been built in the 1930s or 40s especially for transatlantic voyages, were large and expensive to run and may not have appealed fully to the tastes of the one-class 'swinging sixties' cruise passenger. P&O's wonderful *Canberra* of 1961 had given a hint of what the future might look like but, with Cunard's new *QE2* still at the design stage, it would be fair to say that the majority of British cruise ships in the mid-60s were relatively traditional in both appearance and style.

Alexandr Pushkin and her sisters, however, represented something very different. Their sleek modern lines appealed to the eye and their highly competitive fares to the pocket. In addition, the thrill and novelty of experiencing a voyage on board a Soviet ship at a time of such international tension proved an irresistible draw to some middle class British and European passengers. UK bookings were initially handled by Stelp & Leighton Ltd of 9-13 Fenchurch Buildings, London but during the winter of 1968/69 the agency passed to Royal Mail Lines Ltd who at

that time operated the dedicated up-market cruise ship *Andes* and three passenger/cargo combination liners, *Amazon, Aragon* and *Arlanza* that offered a regular UK-South America service. They had offices at 10, Haymarket, London (where a beautiful, illuminated model of *Alexandr Pushkin* was displayed) as well as in Belfast, Birmingham, Glasgow, Liverpool and Manchester and were therefore well-placed to give maximum exposure to the Baltic Steamship Company programmes, which did not compete at all with their own brand. On 21st December 1968 the ship departed on her first 13 night cruise from Tilbury to the Canaries, calling at Las Palmas, Tenerife, Casablanca and Cadiz and Gibraltar for the New Year festivities.

To lure British cruise passengers in large numbers to an unknown Russian ship was always going to be a tall order, and the marketing team at Royal Mail Lines decided to meet the challenge head-on with the 'Welcome aboard' copy for its '*Alexandr Pushkin* ' six-page A4 leaflet:

"ALEXANDR PUSHKIN is a Russian cruise ship. If you expect it to make a difference, you're right. There has seldom been anything like it for value! The crew and cabin staff (many of whom speak excellent English) think of themselves as temporary ambassadors – and with traditional Russian hospitality they'll give you your warmest-ever welcome. The service is excellent and the 330 crew members will do their utmost to spoil you.

On ALEXANDR PUSHKIN everything is designed for your comfort. For instance, she is stabilised and fully air-conditioned to maintain just the right temperature. She's one-class of course, and as she is one of the most modern ships of her size sailing from Britain you get all the touches that make cruising the perfect holiday – everything from a swimming pool to a beauty parlour.

From Christmas to March ALEXANDR PUSHKIN voyages to warmer seas. Sail into the sunshine with us! A cruise on board this beautiful ship, flagship of the Baltic Shipping Company will cost you far less than you ever thought possible. (No 'V' Form needed either: you could keep every penny of your £50 allowance for the summer) This is holiday cruising **you can** afford!"

Having made the point that this was a different type of cruise and that it was cheap – the fares for a fourteen night Canary Island Cruise started at £80 for the minimum four berth cabin grade with washbasin only, rising through £150 for a two berth cabin with shower and toilet, to £215 per person for the highest category two bedded cabin with bath, shower and toilet – the brochure then had to ensure that the old British adage of 'If it's that cheap, it can't be any good' did not apply. There were therefore extensive reassurances regarding the quality of the offering: 'We serve caviar (sic) during every cruise – along with many

У Лукоморья дуб зеленый;

PROGRAMME

M.S. „ALEXANDR PUSHKIN"

Daily program

4

JUNE 20th, 1967

At 8 a.m. North Sea
Distance to Montreal 3360 s.m.

TODAYS EVENTS

8 a.m.	Pre-Breakfast Workout in Gymnasium. «B» deck AFT.
	Deck Games on Sports Decks
	Shuffleboard, Horse Racing, Table Tennis.
10 a.m.	All passengers are requested to collect their passports and Landing Cards at the Information Office.
	Arrival at BREMERHAVEN.
12 noon	Workout in Gymnasium.
	All passengers must be back on board ship.
	Depart BREMERHAVEN.
	Abfahrt von Bremerhaven.
	Afternoon Tea. Dining Room
	Cocktail Hour. Recorded Music.

1st class only — «White Nights» Bar.
Tourist class — «North Palmyra» Cafe
«Penguins» Cafe.

Dancing in the Music Salon. Orest Kandat and His Orchestra.
Bingo in the «White Nights» Lounge (1st Class)
Dancing in «White Nights» Lounge. First Class
Ludmila Gogunina Sings in the «White Nights» Lounge (1st Class)
«White Nights» Bar Open. First Class.

2 a.m. Midnight Snacks.
Mitternachtssnack.

1st class only — «White Nights» Bar.
Tourist class — «North Palmyra» Cafe
«Penguins» Cafe.
«Friendship» Bar.

CINEMA "Aurora" CINEMA

3 p.m. «Our Hermitage» (in Russian).
8 p.m. and 9.45 p.m. «Miss Planetkaia» (in English).
Passengers are requested to refrain from smoking in the cinema hall.

Notices...

IMPORTANT!
Immigration formalities will take place in the Music Salon from 10 a.m. to 11 a.m.
The gangway for transit passengers will be on Promenade Deck.
The gangway for landing passengers will be on Boat Deck.

THE BEST BUYS IN OUR BARS ARE:
A good selection of Russian and foreign spirits is kept in the ship's bars.
Genuine Russian Vodka, Georgian Dry wines, Armenian cognac.
The «Dark caviare — the blackest (blacker than the blackest!) and the tastiest as well in the world...
We advise you to take advantage of the duty free prices on board ship.

DAS BESTE, WAS MAN IN UNSEREN BARS KAUFEN KAN:
Eine grosse Auswahl von russischen und fremden Weinen.
Echte russische Vodka, grusinische Weine, armenischer Cognac und auch schwarzer Kaviar, der am besten schmeckt.
Wir empfehlen unseren Fahrgasten die gebührfreien Einkäufe in unseren Bars zu machen.

Open times for bars and shops during the ship's stay at Bremerhaven.
«Friendship» Bar — from 10 a.m. to 3 p.m.
«Beriozka» Shop — from 10 a.m. to 3 p.m.

WEATHER
At 8 a.m. Wind N 3-4. Air temperature 15-16 C. Sea 2-3.
Barometer 1010-1015 mb.
FORECAST FOR TODAY. Wind N 4. Air temperature 18-19 C. Sea 3.

Daily programmes and menus on board the Baltic Steamship Company's vessels were characterised by their striking and varied artwork. This one was published on board *Alexandr Pushkin* on 20th June 1967. (Richard Bastow)

Guests at a reception on board *Alexandr Pushkin* at Montreal during 1977 include Roger O. Beauchemin (President and Chief Executive of the Port of Montreal 1977–1981) and the Russian Ambassador, Nicholas Beshwaty. (Tony Boemi)

other Russian delicacies'; 'the cuisine on board…is both lavish and delicious'; 'the main swimming pool is heated and surprisingly large'; 'With three decks for sunbathing and 268 spacious and comfortable cabins – literally acres in which to spread yourselves' and 'The night life's lively…exciting Russian Cabaret in the Music Saloon…all the singers and dancers are in fact crew members but for entertainment value they're better than many professionals'.

Some novel sales features were also used to tempt the travelling public. Shark fishing was billed as an attraction on the January 1972 West Indies cruise from Tilbury! Apparently 'for this exciting occasion the ship is stopped in mid-ocean and you're treated to a really thrilling spectacle of

A 1970-71 Winter Sun brochure, marketed by Royal Mail Lines Ltd. (David Trevor Jones

skill and daring'. How the requisite sharks could be guaranteed to appear on cue – in daylight, between meal times and not clashing with the semi finals of the mixed shuffleboard competitions – is not actually explained in the brochure. Still for £135.00 for 26 nights, one couldn't complain!

One memorable aspect of the ship's life which the brochures did not mention was the ship's band. Consisting of a dozen or so smartly-uniformed musicians playing saxophones, trumpets, clarinets, tubas, a big drum and cymbals, the band provided a rousing accompaniment to *Alexandr Pushkin's* arrival at and departure from each port and added greatly to the atmosphere of excitement.

As an insurance against insufficient British passengers embarking at Tilbury to fill the ship on every cruise, *Alexandr Pushkin* always called at Rotterdam to embark/disembark continental European passengers, who were mainly German and Dutch and procured by the general passenger agents in those countries. The typical pattern for a winter sunshine cruise can be seen from the example below:

Day 1: Sat 24th Jan 1970 Tilbury 0800-1900h
British passengers from the previous cruise finally disembark. Continental passengers that joined in Rotterdam on 8 January have time ashore in London for sightseeing and excursions. New British passengers embark for this cruise.

Day 2: Sun 25th Jan 1970 Rotterdam 0800-1300h
Finally disembark previous cruise continental passengers. The new British passengers that joined the previous day have a transit call in Rotterdam for sightseeing and tours. New continental passengers embark.

Day 5: Thu 29th Jan 1970 Las Palmas arrive1600h
Day 7: Sat 31st Jan 1970 Las Palmas sail 0400h
Day 7: Sat 31st Jan 1970 Tenerife 0800-2400h
Day 9: Mon 2nd Feb 1970 Casablanca 0800-2000h
Day 10: Tue 3rd Feb 1970 Gibraltar arrive 0800h
Day 11: Wed 4th Feb 1970 Gibraltar sail 0200h
Day 14: Sat 7th Feb 1970 Tilbury 0800-1900h
British passengers finally disembark. Continental passengers have a transit call in London for sightseeing and excursions. New British passengers embark for the next cruise.

Day 15: Sun 8th Feb 1970 Rotterdam 0800-1300h
Finally disembark previous cruise continental passengers. The new British passengers that joined the previous day have time ashore in

Rotterdam for sightseeing and tours. New continental passengers embark for the next cruise.

So, what did a traveller of the 1960s and 70s actually experience on board? An English passenger, in a postcard home from the Gulf of St. Lawrence, enthused in May 1969 that *Alexandr Pushkin* was 'a simply super ship. Have never seen such variety and quantity of food...service great with much charm...we have a very happy table and Winifred has decided to adopt our steward!' David Trevor Jones, who sailed on one of her sisters, recalls that 'the food was luxurious by domestic Soviet and opulent by today's western standards with sturgeon and caviar appearing regularly, interspersed with borscht and other Russian standards. One afternoon tea memorably included small 'apple' tarts that were actually filled with cabbage....Vodka flowed freely... and there was a complete absence of any licensing laws which prohibited the sale of alcohol to teenagers!'

BALTIC STEAMSHIP COMPANY

M.S. „ALEXANDR PUSHKIN"

M.S. „ALEXANDR PUSHKIN"

BALTIC STEAMSHIP COMPANY

A dinner menu for 8th May 1967 (left) and a lunch menu for 25th June 1967 (right). (Richard Bastow)

DECK PLAN

FULLY AIR CONDITIONED · STABILIZED

THE FLAGSHIP OF
THE BALTIC STEAMSHIP COMPANY
M.S. ALEXANDR PUSHKIN

Alexandr Pushkin's internal layout as built, as illustrated in a deck plan booklet issued during 1967 or 1968. The photographs below show the Music Saloon dance floor and the open Upper Deck or Compass Platform while those opposite feature one of the lobbies with its open, semi-spiral staircases, the Restaurant and the Cinema/Lecture Theatre, together with a selection of cabins. (Richard Clammer)

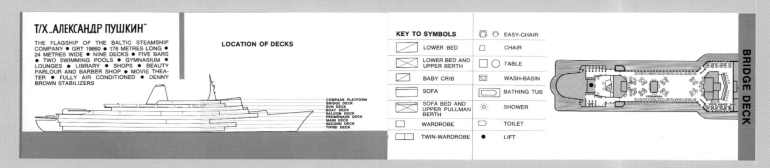

Т/Х „АЛЕКСАНДР ПУШКИН"

THE FLAGSHIP OF THE BALTIC STEAMSHIP COMPANY • GRT 19860 • 176 METRES LONG • 24 METRES WIDE • NINE DECKS • FIVE BARS • TWO SWIMMING POOLS • GYMNASIUM • LOUNGES • LIBRARY • SHOPS • BEAUTY PARLOUR AND BARBER SHOP • MOVIE THEATER • FULLY AIR CONDITIONED • DENNY BROWN STABILIZERS

LOCATION OF DECKS

COMPASS PLATFORM
BRIDGE DECK
SUN DECK
BOAT DECK
SALOON DECK
PROMENADE DECK
MAIN DECK
SECOND DECK
THIRD DECK

KEY TO SYMBOLS

LOWER BED	EASY-CHAIR
LOWER BED AND UPPER BERTH	CHAIR
BABY CRIB	TABLE
SOFA	WASH-BASIN
SOFA BED AND UPPER PULLMAN BERTH	BATHING TUB
WARDROBE	SHOWER
TWIN-WARDROBE	TOILET
	LIFT

BRIDGE DECK

M/S "ALEXANDR PUSHKIN"

DE LUXE STATEROOMS

Nos. 101, 102, 103, 104

Each with private bath, lower beds and telephone

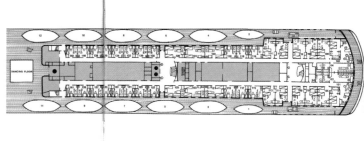

BOAT DECK

M/S "ALEXANDR PUSHKIN"

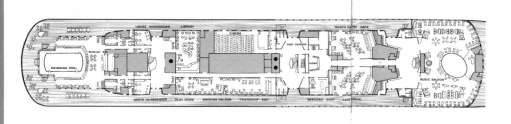

SALOON DECK

26

M/S "ALEXANDR PUSHKIN"

PROMENADE DECK

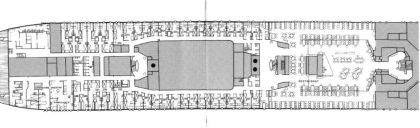

M/S "ALEXANDR PUSHKIN"

MAIN DECK C

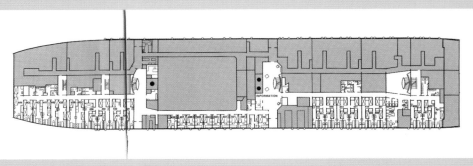

M/S "ALEXANDR PUSHKIN"

SECOND DECK

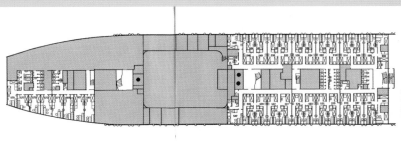

M/S "ALEXANDR PUSHKIN"

THIRD DECK

MOVIE THEATER
(ON THE SALOON DECK)

The ship's interiors, although modern and bright, were relatively dated by western standards and emphatically Soviet in character. Formica was the material of choice for bulkheads, table tops and bunk sides. Much of the furniture sported metal or bent wood frames with minimal upholstery and soft furnishings were sparingly used. The layout of the ship was so completely different from the *Marco Polo* of today that a comparison of her original layout as built and contemporary deck plans makes an absorbing study.

The majority of the ship's public rooms were concentrated on today's Magellan Deck (Deck 8), which was then referred to as the Saloon Deck and did not extend as far forward as in its present configuration. At the forward end was the Music Saloon whose central feature was an oval dance floor backed by a small, wedge-shaped stage decorated with abstract motifs of musical instruments. Around the perimeter of the saloon fixed tables set at right angles to the ship's side and easy chairs created an alcove effect, while the remaining space was provided with a mixture of round and oblong tables, easy chairs and sofas.

Moving aft, two wide doorways led from the music saloon into the forwards lobby and stairwell, with toilets to port and starboard. The original stairways were of a flattened spiral design, with each curving flight cutting sharply back on the ones above and below. The stair rails were of shaped metal capped with plastic-coated steel handrails, the

The shop.
(CMV/ Morgan Van Selman)

treads were uncarpeted and the open design of the stair wells meant that it was possible to peer over the edge and see the entire height of the ship.

From here, passengers passed through a central glazed corridor between the North Palmira Cafe to port and the Cafe Penguin to starboard to a central 'town square' with a kiosk amidships, the post office to port and the Beriozka Shop to starboard. Next came the midships lobby and stairwell, with more toilets and doors leading out onto the partially-enclosed open deck. Aft from here the ship's centre-line was taken up with the engine room casing and the port side by a large cinema / lecture theatre which showed an 'improving' diet of carefully-selected Soviet films in what would be regarded today as extremely austere surroundings.

The through corridor passed down the starboard side of the engine casing passing in turn the Friendship Bar, the Smoking Saloon and a games room, all of which looked outwards onto the open deck and could be split into discrete areas by sliding concertina dividers. The games area was used for a variety of purposes including playing cards, as an additional children's play area or as an area to complete port formalities. Opposite the lounge on the port side and accessed from the aft lobby and stairwell was a large library, fitted with soft seating and well-stocked with 'suitable' books.

Aft of the lobby there was a ladies' hairdresser to port and a gentlemen's hairdresser to starboard. Each adjoined a block of showers and toilets designed to serve the ship's innovative heated swimming pool which occupied the aft end of the saloon deck. The pool was completely enclosed by glazed panels and a sliding glass roof which could be opened when the weather was suitable. The glazed pool area was served by the Rusalka Bar, situated amidships and facing aft, while doors gave access to seating areas on the open deck overlooking the stern.

Another popular feature of the original layout was the large White Nights Lounge which was located on the uppermost deck, then called the Bridge Deck and today known as Navigator Deck (Deck 11). Although fully enclosed, it was fitted with large panoramic windows giving superb sea views, and was capable of serving as a quiet day-time retreat or an intimate night club after dark. Aft of the funnel was an open deck with an enormous skylight, usually kept open for ventilation, through which passengers could view the engine room below. Above the Bridge deck was another spacious open deck area aft of the compass platform to which passengers were sometimes given access and where kennels for dogs were provided. These facilities had to be booked well in advance. Fares for animals were quoted in the brochures, and passengers were required to provide their own baskets and cages to ensure that their pet cats and birds travelled in familiar comfort. Needless to say there were stringent veterinary certification requirements for all animals prior to boarding.

The Promenade Deck – currently Pacific Deck (Deck 7) – was largely occupied by cabins but towards the stern were located a gymnasium to port and a children's play room, complete with slide, roundabout and other play equipment to starboard while the amidships area was occupied by the base of the swimming pool. On the open fantail deck was a large children's paddling pool. Further forward, facing the forward lobby and stairwell, was the ship's information desk.

Almost the only public room which occupied its current position was the restaurant. This was located just forward of mid-ships on Main Deck C, now Atlantic Deck (Deck 6). The suspended ceilings, recessed fluorescent lighting and formica walls were relieved by some attractive murals, modern open metal-work dividing screens, and plants. The wooden chairs were painted black with tan leather-look upholstery and, set against white table cloths, the whole effect was light and pleasing. Right aft, on the starboard side of the same deck, were the unusually large, well-equipped hospital, operating theatre and 'ambulance room'.

Cabin accommodation was situated on five different decks and, although far too austere for today's cruise passenger, was actually far more varied than has sometimes been acknowledged. The best grade cabins were located highest up, on the Boat Deck which forms today's Amundsen Deck (Deck 9). Right forward overlooking the bows were two

de-luxe staterooms, cabin numbers 101-102, which benefitted from separate day rooms, sleeping cabins and bathrooms. Next to these were two single cabins, both at de-luxe cabin rates. Aft of these came the spacious cabins 105-114 and the slightly smaller 121-126 all of which also sported twin beds. The remaining twenty one cabins had twin bunk beds, but every cabin on the Boat Deck enjoyed a private, en-suite toilet and shower. Right aft, on the open section of the deck, was a dance floor laid over the hatch covers to the aft hold. If cargo needed to be embarked the floor could simply be removed and the hold serviced by the two large deck cranes provided!

The Promenade Deck, now Pacific Deck (Deck 7) was one of *Alexandr Pushkin's* more popular features as each and every one of the seventy eight cabins enjoyed an outside view onto a glass-enclosed promenade which ran right around the ship and allowed passengers to take their daily constitutionals whilst sheltered from the ravages of the North Atlantic weather. Those aft of amidships had private facilities and twin beds, while those forward had bunk beds and a wash basin, but no toilet or shower. Toilet and shower blocks to service these cabins were located along on the inboard sides of the long access corridors.

On Main Deck C (Atlantic Deck 6) aft of the restaurant were another forty-nine twin or four berth cabins, all with bunks and wash basins and served by inboard bathroom blocks. Further down, the Second Deck, now Baltic Deck (Deck 5) had crew spaces to port but forty-three more passenger cabins to starboard. Lowest still, the Third Deck (Caribic Deck 4) contained forty-seven more cabins amidships and a further eight right aft, none with private facilities. Many of the cabins on the lowest three

Two young girls enjoying themselves in the children's paddling pool at the aft end of the Promenade Deck, in January 1971. Both of them developed such a love for the ship that they later went on to work for CTC! (Meriel Lowe)

The pool and Rusalka bar, seen after dark (CMV/ Morgan Van Selman)

The library. (CMV/Morgan Van Selman)

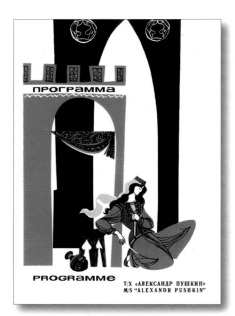

Programme cover (above) and Menu cover (below) from 1971. (Meriel Lowe)

decks were capable of being configured as two or four berth accommodation, while their robust, wipe-clean finishes and generous seating areas would have allowed them to absorb large numbers of troops if the ship was ever required for military purposes

The fact that the ship had also been designed for potential dual use as a fast troop ship and military transport in times of conflict, was reflected in several aspects of her design which have already been mentioned. Behind the scenes she had unusually large food preparation and provision storage areas, and at least one hold was fitted with a lift. More obvious to passengers travelling on board were the six large deck cranes which were designed not only to service the various holds but also to be capable of lifting heavy military equipment or additional boats on board. When the ship was alongside, the sharp-eyed may also have noticed the large side doors in the ship's sides below the fo'c's'le. A purpose-built ramp could be deployed allowing cars to be driven on board during civilian service, or a selection of military vehicles if required. Finally, her unusually wide internal alleyways and corridors had all been designed specifically to allow soldiers in full combat kit to move rapidly around the ship two abreast. Given her standard passenger capacity of 750 and the fact that she was given provision for 500 more 'cabinless' or deck passengers, it is clear that she would have been capable of moving at least 1250 troops at speed over long distances.

The number of cars which could be carried is also open to some dispute. Some sources say 23, some 30 and yet others 50. The size of the cars involved would, of course, make a difference, but the remainder of the discrepancy may be explained by the fact that vehicles could be carried either in the hold or as deck cargo. It therefore seems likely that 23 or so may have been accommodated down below, while others crossed the Atlantic lashed on deck and exposed to salt spray, an experience which cannot have improved the subsequent longevity of their bodywork! Fares for the carriage of vehicles were fixed by the north Atlantic Passenger Steamship Conference and in 1968, for example, the rate for a car weighing under 3,500lbs (1587kg) was quoted as US$350 (then £110) from Montreal to any European port.

During the 1970s each of the 'Russian Poets' received a major refit to bring them more in line with the standards expected of modern cruise liners. *Alexandr Pushkin's* turn came in 1975 and she emerged from the shipyard with improved facilities, an increased gross tonnage of 20,502 and a slightly altered profile.

The most obvious visual change was to the forward end of her superstructure. Her Saloon and Boat decks had both been extended further forward, creating three tiers in place of the former two and slightly spoiling her classic profile. The forward hold and two of the heavy deck cranes had been removed, reducing her cargo capacity but creating an enormous volume of new space for improved facilities. The Music Saloon was greatly enlarged, extending both forward and upwards into the new superstructure. The dance floor was made bigger, the whole saloon remodelled and freshly furnished, and two sets of curving stairs now swept aloft to a new upper bar from which drinkers could look down on the dancers below. Further aft, the popular 'Penguin' and 'North Palmyra' bars were extended and modernised.

On the Boat Deck the former de luxe staterooms were absorbed into a large new lounge which occupied the extended superstructure. The staterooms were replaced by four new ones named Tatjana, Natasha, Olga and Anna, situated amidships on the Promenade Deck . On the same deck several forward cabins were remodelled, some inside cabins created and the former gymnasium area replaced by additional cabins. A new gymnasium, massage room and sauna were on the former open deck aft, the children's paddling pool disappeared and a new open-air pool was constructed on the site of the former dance floor/cargo hatch at the aft end of the Boat Deck. All the cabins on the Promenade Deck were given private facilities, but those on the three lowest decks remained unaltered, still served by the inboard bathroom blocks. The open deck areas towards the aft end of the Saloon Deck were plated in while, up on the Bridge Deck, the White Nights Lounge received a major make-over but continued to feature 'Gennady Pavlov and his Orchestra' each night at 11pm.The somewhat stern appearance of Gennady and his boys was quite misleading and strict tempo ballroom dancing was out of the question as Gennady's band was one of the finest jazz combos in the USSR.

In her new guise, the improved *Alexandr Pushkin* continued with her familiar pattern of summer service on the Leningrad to North America transatlantic run, interspersed with short cruises and full-time cruising during the rest of the year. Clever scheduling of the two-ship transatlantic service also permitted a programme of cruises to be offered from Montreal. In 1977, for example, having arrived from Leningrad on 21st July, *Alexandr Pushkin* immediately embarked on a series of eight cruises. The shorter of these, varying from six to nine days in duration, took her to a selection of Canadian destinations including Quebec, the Saguenay River, Gaspe, St. Pierre Miquelon, St John's (Newfoundland), Sydney (Nova Scotia), Isle de la Madeleine and Charlottetown. The 14 day cruise went via Quebec to Bagotville and Bermuda and, most exotic of all, the 20 day trip went as far south as Bermuda, Nassau and the politically-daring destination of Cuba. Having returned from the final cruise on 9th September, the ship then picked up her transatlantic schedule and departed eastbound on 21st September.

While *Alexandr Pushkin* was busy on her Canadian cruising season, *Mikhail Lermontov* maintained a Leningrad -New York service. The Soviets also saw an opportunity to earn more foreign currency by offering 15 day cruises from either New York or Montreal to the USSR, with the option of either using the ship as a hotel in Leningrad (at a cost of $45 per night, full board) for two days' sightseeing with an Intourist guide before the return sailing, or an option to spend six days in the USSR before returning to North America by air. Organised visits were offered to Kiev and Moscow and extended tours were available to Samarkand, Tashkent, Tbilisi and Odessa. With a wide range of highly-competitive student, emigrant, group, excursion and other fares on offer and the possibility of travelling between any of the ports on the schedule, this proved to be a very attractive and rather exotic offering.

With the demand for transatlantic voyages decreasing and the number of cruise passengers beginning to increase, it was timely that, in 1979, Baltic Shipping Company should make a commitment to cruising by securing charters for its four main vessels on the British and German markets. *Mikhail Lermontov* and *Mikhail Kalinin* were placed with CTC Lines to operate out of the United Kingdom with predominately British passengers whilst *Alexandr Pushkin* and *Estonia* were chartered to Transocean Tours in Bremen to offer an exclusive German cruise experience.

Alexandr Pushkin still had a summer sailing schedule from

Leningrad to Montreal but in 1979 there were just two round trip sailings. At this point she was one of only three liners remaining on the transatlantic run, the others being the Polish *Stefan Batory* and Cunard's *Queen Elizabeth 2*. External factors, following the Soviet invasion of Afghanistan in December 1979 and the mass boycott of the 1980 Olympic Games in Moscow, meant that 1980 was the final year of her transatlantic operations. She did however complete a number of cruises for Transocean from Bremerhaven.

A pattern for the next few years was set and itineraries were suitably varied with long winter voyages and shorter sailings for the rest of the year. The Baltic, Norway and Spitzbergen had always been popular

A 1977 ticket cover. (Richard Bastow)

A diploma issued to a junior passenger on 26th February 1972 to mark the completion of a 27 night cruise. (Meriel Lowe)

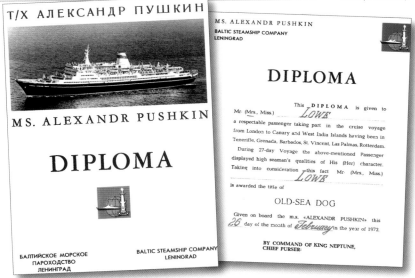

31

The mechanical hoist and hull doors in use as a car is loaded into the forward hold. (David Trevor-Jones)

A 1974 shore excursions leaflet. (Richard Bastow)

destinations for German passengers and these cruises were interspersed with southbound sailings to the Atlantic Islands, West Africa and into the Mediterranean. From 1967, when Transocean had first been appointed as general passenger agents in West Germany for the Baltic Shipping Company, through until 1979, the German passengers invariably had to tolerate a dual language operation, and all the irritations which that brings, as British passengers were also embarked at Tilbury.

However the exclusive charter of the ship by Transocean signified that the every cruise could be a purely German product in terms of language, menus, entertainment and shore excursions. This made life easier for everyone on board and *Alexandr Pushkin's* reputation soared, with huge numbers of passengers returning year after year. In 1982, Transocean extended its fleet with the additional charter of the 550 passenger capacity *Odessa,* and vessel which was only eight years old and whose 273 cabins were all outside with private shower and toilet.

In 1982 the travel writer Gavin Young, who had previously written a best-selling account of his ship-hopping travels from Greece to China, *Slow Boats to China,* was making his way back to England again and, finding himself stranded in Tahiti, managed to book a single passage on board the *Alexandr Pushkin* across the Pacific to Callao in Peru. His book, *Slow Boats Home,* contains an extremely entertaining account of his experiences as the sole Englishman among a ship full of well-established German round-the -world voyagers and gives a well-observed and affectionate account of many of the characters on board, including Capt. Vitaly Segal.

The CTC Cruises fleet cruising out of the UK at this time consisted of the newly-refurbished *Mikhail Lermontov* and a recently refitted and improved *Kareliya* partnered by the smaller *Mikhail Kalinin*. All three ships could offer en-suite facilities. In line with changing aspirations, passengers were becoming less inclined to accept washbasin-only cabins and the accompanying communal shower and toilet facilities.

It was this cabin accommodation issue that was partly the reason for the next major development in the career of *Alexandr Pushkin*. From the total of 262 cabins, only 110 of them could offer private facilities. With passenger expectations changing in Europe it was decided that the ship would be more appropriately placed in another market. In 1984, she was

transferred from the ownership of Baltic Shipping Company, Leningrad, to that of the Far Eastern Shipping Company (FESCO) based in Vladivostok.

It was decided to mark the handover in some style and on the 30th August 1984, she made her last call at Tilbury, setting off on a grand 42 night voyage to the Far East and Japan. A limited edition print of the ship signed by the Master, Vitaly Sigel, and key members of the ship's company was presented to each passenger upon their disembarkation in Hong Kong and a couple of days later a very sad Baltic Shipping crew handed *Alexandr Pushkin* over to their Far East Shipping Company counterparts.

With the lifting of the Australian government ban on Aeroflot and Morpasflot which had been imposed in reaction to the Soviet invasion of Afghanistan, the 'other market' was revealed as the younger cruising element that had been sailing very successfully on Russian ships out of Australia prior to that embargo. Therefore, on the 21st December, 1984, *Alexandr Pushkin* became the first Soviet passenger vessel for almost four years to enter the 'Heads' of Sydney Harbour to begin a new chapter cruising with CTC Cruises passengers out of Australia. The ship herself

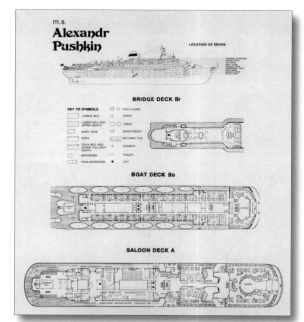

A deck plan showing the alterations carried out in 1975. (David Trevor-Jones)

was relatively unchanged under FESCO, although most noticeably the Saloon Deck swimming pool had had its glass canopy removed and become an open air pool. The two 'twin bars', formerly the 'Penguin' and 'North Palmyra' had been renamed 'Golden Horn' and 'Vladivostok' respectively and a CTC office, for the Cruise Director and his staff, and an indoor activity room replaced the Games Room and Smoking Saloon of BSC days. To complete the nomenclature, the 'Russalka Bar' by the lido became, somewhat unimaginatively, the 'Lido Bar'.

She was joined in that first season by her sister ship *Mikhail Lermontov,* which also operated a short season from Sydney between line voyages from and to the UK, and therefore the two North Atlantic twins were reunited in a more tropical setting. There were emotional scenes when the two ships met up in Noumea, New Caledonia on 25th February, 1985.

Alexandr Pushkin, was slightly more popular than her younger sister in that first year of operation in Australia. Her cheaper non-facility cabins sold well, particularly the four berths, appealing to the younger crowd of passengers that she used to attract. In fact certain sailings were designated 'Fun and Sun Cruises' exclusively for the 18 – 35 age group. A 1986 Australian brochure expounded 'it's a non-stop floating rage, every day, every night for the 18 to 35s. No kids or oldies on board to worry about, but more guys and girls than you can handle.' (!)

As the ship was based in Vladivostok, she often positioned at the start of each season or repositioned at the season end with cruises sailing from or arriving into Hong Kong. This gave CTC opportunities to add in air and land arrangements which could make a potentially difficult to sell 'open-jaw' voyage into a spectacular inclusive tour. In 1987 for instance,

Alexandr Pushkin at sea showing the alterations made to her forward superstructure in 1975 (FotoFlite)

The modified interior of the forward lounge or Music Saloon, showing the two sets of stairs sweeping up to the new balcony and bar above. (CMV / Morgan Van Selman)

The commemorative print which was presented to passengers at the end of the voyage to Hong Kong. (Richard Bastow)

Dancers are depicted on this large-format publicity card, one of several issued during the early 1970s. (Richard Bastow)

A Transocean Tours' German language brochure for **Alexandr Pushkin's** valedictory 42-night sailing from Europe to Hong Kong. (Richard Bastow)

FERNOST
Kreuzfahrt
mit Rückflug oder Rückreise mit der
TRANSSIBIRISCHEN Eisenbahn
Lufthansa

Indien / Ceylon / Malaysia
Thailand / Philippinen / Hongkong
Japan: Tokio, Nagasaki

»Alexandr Pushkin«

Drei Strecken stehen zur Auswahl:
1. Gesamtreise Bremerhaven–Nachodka–Frankfurt   ab DM 6580,–
2. Bremerhaven–Hongkong–Frankfurt   ab DM 6060,–
3. Bremerhaven–Nagasaki–Frankfurt   ab DM 7990,–

Veranstalter: *Transocean-Tours*

Alexandr Pushkin and *Mikhail Lermontov* illuminated during a winter sunshine cruise, 1975. (Richard Bastow)

the ship finished her season by sailing from Sydney on 19th August, reaching Hong King on 5th September having called at Madang in Papua New Guinea, and Cebu and Manila in the Philippines. Upon disembarkation there was a two night hotel stay in Hong Kong and then a flight on to the UK arriving into London Gatwick on 8th September. In the advertised fares that started from AU$ 2,370.00 (then the sterling equivalent was £1,044.00), a return air ticket from London back to Australia valid for up to nine months was also included.

The CTC Cruises itineraries in the high season – December to March – generally featured the nearer South Pacific ports in Fiji, Vanuatu and New Caledonia in cruise durations of ten to fourteen nights. The geography meant that any shorter duration would reduce the ports of call down to just two or three calls.

Longer sailings were more occasional but would go as far across the Pacific as Tahiti. A 25 night cruise in February 1987 for instance sailed on a route from Sydney that took in Noumea (New Caledonia), Papeete (Tahiti), Bora Bora (French Polynesia), Apia (Western Samoa), Nukualofa (Tonga), and Auckland (New Zealand). To give some idea as to the huge distances travelled, there were six days at sea between Noumea and Papeete – not that dissimilar to her old Transatlantic days. Later that year an autumn sailing of

39 nights visited Japan (Nagasaki and Yokohama) as well as China (Qingdao) and also included calls in Hong Kong, the Philippines, Papua New Guinea (Madang and Rabaul), and Cairns en route back to Sydney.

The sea days proliferated throughout most of the Australian itineraries which suited the clientele who were extremely active around the ship and *Alexandr Pushkin's* ample sports areas were probably used more than ever before.

By 1989 however, it was becoming increasingly obvious that she was in urgent need of further modernisation and upgrading. Plans were laid to increase capacity and convert all cabins to private facilities, but unfortunately some serious technical problems were revealed in the surveys. The Far Eastern Shipping Company reluctantly decided to sell the vessel and CTC's involvement with this most popular and much loved ship, which had started in 1975 when it gained the Morpasflot General Passenger Agency, came to an end. On the 6th February 1990, she was laid up in Singapore and brokers worldwide were notified that she was available.

A typical page from a 1986-87 CTC Australian cruise brochure, clearly showing the target market. (Richard Bastow)

Alexandr Pushkin arriving at Sydney, Australia. (Richard Bastow)

At Helsinki, Finland, 9th August 2007. (Ian Boyle, Simplon Postcards)

MARCO POLO – FROM POET TO EXPLORER

Given the political turmoil of the time, the urgent need for foreign currency and the fact that shipping lines such as the Far Eastern Shipping Company were grappling with the challenges of operating in a privatised, free market environment rather than under centralised state control, it would have been unsurprising if *Alexandr Pushkin's* career had quietly come to an end. Happily, however, this was not the case. On 8th July 1991 Lloyds List reported that the ship had been sold to a London-based company Shipping & General Ltd, owned by Gerry Herrod, founder of Ocean Cruise Lines which he had sold during 1990 to the French company Paquet Lines for a reported $100 million. Mr Herrod was now in the process of setting up a new cruise company called Orient Lines and decided that *Alexandr Pushkin* was the ideal vessel for his purposes.

Because he intended to employ the ship on a new style of adventurous expedition/destination cruising in Far Eastern waters, he gave her the highly-appropriate new name of *Marco Polo*. She was re-registered in the Bahamas and, as soon as a number of repairs were completed to prepare her for the voyage, she set sail for Greece to commence a major refit.

The ship went first to Piraeus where initial gutting of the interiors took place. She was then towed to the Neorian Shipyard on the Greek Island of Syros where structural steel modifications were carried out and her main engines and auxiliaries underwent full re-conditioning by their original manufacturer, Sulzer Ltd. The survey had revealed that one engine had a cracked foundation plate, so it had to be lifted and the plate replaced. This process was not without its tensions as Greek shipyards were undergoing a difficult transition from state to private ownership and there was much unrest among the workforce. The Neorian yard was occupied by protesting workers and lay idle for over a month but, by the end of the year, the first stage of the work had been completed and the ship was moved to the Perama shipyard zone near Piraeus.

The main Perama shipyards – Avlis, Nafsi and Eleusis – had developed a reputation for working together on large jobs which might have been beyond the capacity of any individual yard, and this approach was adopted for *Marco Polo*. Avlis had already led the successful conversion of several former ferries into cruise ships, so the combined yards were in a good position to embark on what was to prove a mammoth, two-and-a-half year task. In order to provide facilities for managing this massive project Orient Lines purchased the *Hansiatic*, a small passenger ship which had previously operated between Bremerhaven and Helgoland, and moored her beside the *Marco Polo* to be used as an office and accommodation for the naval architects, interior designers and other project managers.

Marco Polo was entirely gutted and under the supervision of the respected Danish naval architects Knud E.Hansen and interior designers Michael and Agni Katzourakis, completely new interiors were created within the familiar 1965 hull. The forward superstructure was lengthened again to permit the creation of an extended show lounge and the three upper decks were extended further aft and remodelled to include a new bar, a fitness centre, beauty salon and internet cafe plus three jacuzzi whirl pools and a large sunbathing area on the new top deck. The deck houses on the latter were rebuilt in aluminium to save weight and

With her hull shot-blasted, ***Marco Polo*** lays in the Greek shipyard, June 1993. (Meriel Lowe)

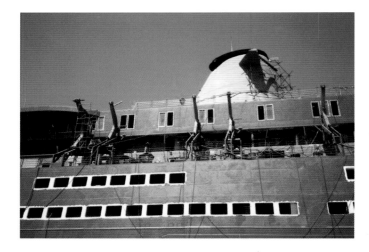

New window openings and upper deck have been installed and work is about to begin on increasing the height of the funnel, 14th June 1993. (Meriel Lowe)

extended abaft the funnel to provide a helicopter landing pad and refuelling station. Internally the upper deck was extensively remodelled. The bridge was rebuilt to include all necessary state-of-the art navigational and safety equipment together with a new radio room and improved officers' accommodation while, further aft, new passenger cabins were installed. These alterations added to the bulk of the ship, so the funnel was heightened to keep everything in perfect proportion.

One fascinating story from the time of the refit relates to the ship's radio room. Behind the bridge was a fully-equipped radio room such as one would expect to find in any large passenger ship but as the refit progressed another identical space was discovered further aft on the same deck and disguised as an officer's cabin. Russian officers who had helped to deliver the ship confirmed old Cold War suspicions by explaining that this secret room belonged to the KGB whose operatives had always sailed onboard *Alexandr Pushkin* and other Soviet merchant ships. Also discovered were an ancient but operational offset printing machine of a type not used in the West since the 1950s, a large library of leather-bound Russian classics translated into English and a menagerie of snakes in the disused provision store rooms!

Internally, only the ship's engines, the restaurant, galley, lower swimming pool and certain service areas remained in their original positions. Most of the remodelled public rooms (which will be described in detail in Chapter 4) were still located on the former Saloon Deck, while others were located at the aft end of the two extended decks above. The spiral staircases of Soviet days would not have complied with

forthcoming SOLAS (The International Convention for the Safety of Life at Sea) regulations and were replaced with new enclosed ones of a more conventional, square design and lifts were installed between all decks.

Because the ship was intended to operate for most of the year in Far Eastern waters, Herrod commissioned a whole range of oriental artworks and sculpture to adorn the public spaces and, complimented by the muted tones chosen for walls, carpets and fabric, these gave the new interiors a wonderfully tranquil, restful ambience.

New cabins, of fifteen different categories from standard inside twin to de-luxe ocean view, were created on seven different decks. Averaging about 13 sq.m., they varied in size from 10. 21 sq.m. to 44.96 sq.m. and all were en suite, air conditioned and elegantly decorated. The largest number were concentrated on the former Promenade Deck which previously had cabins facing onto a glass-enclosed wrap-around walkway. All of these were stripped out and rebuilt to accommodate outside cabins with large windows in the hull, two fore-and-aft corridors and back-to-back inside cabins in the centre of the ship. A total of 800 passengers could be accommodated in 6 suites and 419 cabins, 288 of which were outside.

Behind the scenes, new Denny Brown stabilizers were added, and four new auxiliary diesel generators were fitted. The ship was brought up to international regulatory standards by fitting new fire detection, alarm and extinguishing systems, fitting new watertight and fire zone doors, and installing new lifeboats, davits, life rafts and other safety equipment. An extensive suite of pollution control and abatement equipment was installed, including both waste water plants and state-of-the-art solid waste sorters, compactors and incinerators. Wiring was renewed, new galleys, pantries, fridges and freezers fitted and new toilets installed throughout the accommodation. The former automobile garage with its side loading doors and ramp, was reconfigured to handle and stow a small fleet of inflatable zodiac boats that would land passengers on remote shores while the new helipad allowed a scouting helicopter to be embarked while the ship was in Antarctic waters. Explorer Eric Linblad provided guidance on these features. The hospital was relocated to amidships on the current Baltic Deck and many other crew and service facilities were remodelled. The ship's gross tonnage had now increased to 22,080 tons.

The original electric bow thruster unit from Soviet days had been fed by long cables running from the main switchboard in the engine room to a huge electric motor fixed on top of the thruster unit. It was discovered that this was so power-hungry that the Russians had been forced to stop the operation of the main galley and close down the ship's air-conditioning systems whenever the ship was manoeuvring! To resolve

A scene of organised chaos on the after end of Magellan Deck. Timber, reels of electrical cable and other materials are stacked everywhere while two shipyard workers concentrate on tiling the pool area. (Meriel Lowe)

Work underway on rebuilding the ship's interior showing: Marco's Bistro (above), the Boutique/Shop area (below) and a stairway and the bridge (bottom). (Meriel Lowe)

A publicity postcard issued by Orient Lines before *Marco Polo* entered service, showing an artist's impression of her passing the Hong Kong skyline. (Meriel Lowe)

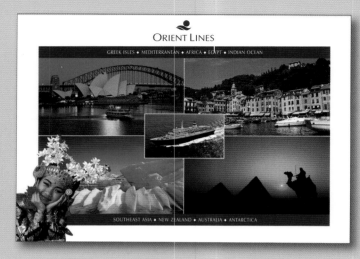

An Orient Lines composite postcard showing a variety of the ship's intended destinations. (Ian Boyle, Simplon Postcards)

A NEW ERA IN DESTINATIONAL CRUISING

A NEW ERA IN DESTINATIONAL CRUISING

A selection of postcards bearing Orient Lines marketing slogan "A new era in destination cruising" and showing *Marco Polo* in various exotic, Far Eastern settings. (Ian Boyle, Simplon Postcards)

the problem a separate generator was purchased to provide direct power and mounted above the bow thruster, in a new 'mini engine room' which required its own fire enclosure and exhaust outlets.

The rebuild reportedly cost $60 million but seems to have met Gerry Herrod's requirements exactly. What emerged from the shipyard was a combination of luxurious modern accommodation designed for the premium 'destination cruising' market, packaged within a shapely, stable, ice-strengthened hull and the elegant profile of a classic ocean liner. Cruise trade magazines were highly complimentary, commenting on the fine sea views from her public rooms, her extensive open decks and superb facilities which provided a level of comfort only then becoming available on far larger ships.

A strike in the shipyard delayed *Marco Polo's* inaugural voyage from 30th October until 19th November 1993. Thereafter she sailed on Orient Lines' first advertised cruise from Mombasa to South Africa and settled in to her exotic and original programme which took her to a wide variety of interesting and seldom-visited ports in south-east Asia. During her time with Orient Lines the ship cruised from Mombasa, Singapore, Sydney, Bali, Auckland, Christchurch, Hong Kong, Bankok, Cape Town and called at a host of locations in the Indian Ocean, South Pacific and Java Sea. Excursions ashore included safaris and other unusual activities. The cuisine on board was said to be far superior to that on similarly-priced cruises and the original menus were devised by Los Angeles chef Wolfgang Puck.

During the southern summer from December to February, *Marco Polo* left the Indian Ocean and offered a number of adventure cruises from Buenos Aires and Ushuaia to Antarctica where passengers experienced the thrill of navigating amongst floating ice and landing on remote shores in the ship's Zodiac inflatables which were launched from

Marco Polo's Antarctic cruises were a major and adventurous element of Orient Line's programme. These stunning images, although taken during the ship's time with Orient Lines, were later edited to show the funnel colours of her next operator, Transocean Tours. (CMV)

their store beneath the foredeck using two modern, hydraulic cranes. A helicopter was embarked on the helipad abaft the funnel for these cruises and was used for spotting whales and other wildlife and guiding the ship or her Zodiacs through the ice.

Unfortunately, the initial season of Antarctic cruises did not prove commercially successful. Environmental regulations limited the passenger numbers to 400, which was only half the ship's normal complement, and in order to protect the fragile ecosystem only 100 could be put ashore at any one time. The Antarctic was thus dropped from

Orient Lines' 1994-95 schedules, but revived in 1996-97 using a slightly revised pricing structure.

Since it was suspected that the demand for Far East cruises might not be robust enough to support the ship all-year-round, Orient Lines announced the introduction of cruises in the eastern Mediterranean from May to October 1996. Unfortunately, this too was fraught with difficulties and *Marco Polo* was refused entry to Piraeus during the first voyage of the eastern Mediterranean cruise programme. The Greek Federation of Seamen organized a protest, claiming that Orient Lines' policy of employing Scandinavian officers and Filipino crew violated Greek cabotage laws which forbad the embarkation/disembarkation of passengers in Greek ports by a foreign ships. Tug crews and port pilots boycotted her and the Harbour Master allegedly refused to allow her to enter the port. This was all despite the fact that during the previous month the Minister of Shipping, Kosmas Sfryriou, had reversed a ruling by the Greek Ministry of Merchant Marine against Orient Lines on the question of cabotage compliance and had declared Orient Lines' Piraeus–Istanbul and Piraeus–Barcelona cruises to be legal.

The dispute continued to escalate through the next three months. In late May, angry Greek seafarers clashed with coast guard personnel assigned to protect the ship and the crew but, by mid-June, a temporary injunction allowed the ship to return to business on its scheduled itinerary. In view of the huge amount of income that *Marco Polo's* refit had so recently brought to the port of Piraeus, the whole situation had a certain bitter irony.

Eventually a compromise was engineered and Orient Lines announced that during the summer of 1997 *Marco Polo* would concentrate on the Western Mediterranean, but that they would maintain their market presence in Greece by chartering in the 500-passenger, Greek-flagged *Ocean Majesty*. Peace had finally broken out!

Having built up a loyal and enthusiastic following for her innovative cruises, *Marco Polo* established herself as a popular market leader and soon attracted the acquisitive gaze of the huge Norwegian Cruise Line (NCL)

which made an offer that her owners could not refuse and absorbed both Orient Line and the ship into their fleet during 1998. In 1999 NCL itself was acquired by the rapidly-expanding Hong Kong-based Star Cruises, which has since gone on to become one of the largest global cruise lines in the world, with almost complete domination of the Asia-Pacific market.

Initially Orient Lines continued to be marketed as a distinct brand by NCL and there was no outward change to *Marco Polo's* pattern of operation. Between 2000 and 2003, however, she was joined by the *Crown Odyssey* and in 2001 it was suggested that a third ship, the *Ocean Voyager (ex SuperStar Aries)* would be added during the following year. In the event, partly due to the effects of 9/11 which resulted in far less Americans travelling abroad, this plan was abandoned, *Crown Odyssey* returned to the NCL fleet and *Marco Polo* soldiered on alone. However, it was becoming increasingly apparent that neither the ship nor her style of operation fitted easily into the Star Cruises' business model, so a decision was made to discontinue the Orient Lines brand from 2008 and offer *Marco Polo* for sale.

It is an interesting aside that the Orient Lines brand was later purchased by the Origin Cruise Group, owned by Wayne Heller, who stated his intention of re-starting the operation with several second-hand ships. By a strange co-incidence his first acquisition was the *Maksim Gorkiy* (ex. *Hamburg*) which back in 1974 had been purchased by the Soviets as a substitute for building the sixth and final member of the 'Russian Poet' class. *Maksim Gorkiy* was due to enter service for the re-born Orient Line in April 2009 as the *Marco Polo II* but the plan never came to fruition. An economic crisis intervened, the refit never materialised and the ship was sent to the ship breakers in January 2009.

Marco Polo, meanwhile, had been sold on 4th June 2007 to the Greek-owned Global Maritime Group but chartered back to Orient Lines to allow them to complete their published programme of cruises to Antarctica and South America. The final cruise terminated at Lisbon on 22nd March 2008 and following the disembarkation of her passengers on the following morning, she was formally delivered to her new owners. The Global Maritime Group had already prepared a long term charter for the vessel to the German Transocean Tours. She replaced the *Arielle* within their fleet and promptly commenced operating in April 2008 from the UK, where she once again became a familiar sight at the Tilbury Landing Stage, which now bore the grander title of The London International Cruise Terminal. It will be recalled that Transocean Tours had been the West German agents for the Baltic Steamship Company between 1966 and 1979, and were therefore familiar with the ship in her previous incarnation as the *Alexandr Pushkin*.

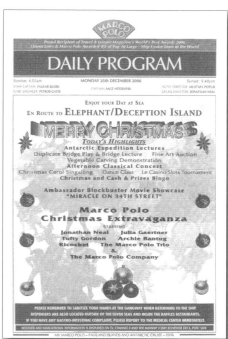

The daily programme for Christmas day 2006 while *Marco Polo* was at sea, en route from the Falkland Islands to Elephant and Deception Islands. (Richard Bastow)

Passengers on board *Marco Polo* enjoying the spectacular Antarctic scenery. (CMV)

Marco Polo arriving at Dover. (John Mavin)

Marco Polo at sea in Transocean livery. (CMV)

THE ADVENT OF CRUISE & MARITIME VOYAGES

As the reader will already have gathered, the relationship between the owner, charterer, operator and agent for any particular cruise liner can be a complex matter. This chapter therefore describes how *Marco Polo's* current operation under Cruise & Maritime Voyages came about.

It will be recalled that back in the 1970s and 80s when the ship was still the *Alexandr Pushkin*, many of her sailings had been marketed through Transocean Tours or the Charter Travel Club under its two guises as CTC Lines and CTC Cruises, all of which were Soviet owned. Among the staff at CTC's London office at 1, Lower Regent Street were Richard Bastow who had joined as a reservations clerk in June 1976, Chris Coates who joined the Passenger Department in 1983 and Sharon Presslie who was appointed as the P.A to the Directors two months later.

By 1995 they had risen through the ranks to become Managing Director, Sales Director and Fleet Product Manager respectively. They had witnessed the various corporate changes that the company had undergone leading up to the disintegration of the Soviet Union in 1991 and subsequently experienced the difficulties of running the under-financed business under its new Ukrainian identity, in the face of new competition from operators such as Airtours and Thomson which added to that from the established cruise lines. By the end of the year all three had departed from the company, taking with them 40 years of cumulative experience. Their involvement with the cruise industry was, however, very far from over.

In May 1996, Richard Bastow teamed up again with Chris Coates to establish Cruise & Maritime Services (CMS) in Dartford, Kent and Sharon Bastow (neé Presslie), joined the embryonic setup four months later. The initial business plan was to provide representation

CTC Lines' offices at 1, Lower Regent Street, London which they occupied from 1975 until 1997. Many major shipping lines had their offices in this prestigious area and this particular building had previously accommodated the Blue Star Line. (Richard Bastow)

A group of travel agents and Royal Mail Line employees on board *Alexandr Pushkin* during a familiarisation cruise from Tilbury to Rotterdam during February 1974. Richard Bastow, who went on to be co-founder of CMV, is fourth from the right.(Richard Bastow)

Early morning in the beautiful Stockholm Archipelago, 15th June 2012. (Richard Clammer)

Arielle off Dubrovnik. (Neven Jercovic)

for cruise lines or operators that did not have a presence in the United Kingdom. However opportunities soon developed to act as charter brokers, matching suitable vessels to the needs of various UK and European tour operators. Entertainment and shore excursion divisions were established and these services were made available to every CMS charterer.

The mainstream cruise lines, particularly Celebrity, Norwegian Cruise Line and Princess Cruises had, however, commenced extensive new building programmes and this meant that the traditional CMS charterers were able to place large groups of passengers on pre-scheduled cruises rather than charter ships themselves. This had a significant financial benefit for the charterers but, needless to say, an equally significant but adverse effect on the CMS's business. To combat this development, the company reverted to its original business model and, from 2003, represented overseas cruise operators such as the Arcalia Shipping Company/Classic International Cruises of Portugal, Cyprus-based Louis Cruises and, significantly, Transocean Tours of Bremen in the UK market.

Drawing on their extensive collective experience, the senior management of CMS were confident enough to propose programmes of no-fly cruises from the UK to be operated by each of these companies under their own names. The under-used London International Cruise Terminal at Tilbury (which had been the base for CTC's earlier operations and which was conveniently close to CMS's Dartford office) was selected as the home port for each of these programmes.

However, operating classic, older, smaller ships successfully in the face of competition from established brand names and newly-built, larger vessels meant that CMS had to be a little creative in its thinking in order to fill the ships for their owners and they concluded that, if you could not always get the market to come to the ship, there might be greater success if the ship was taken to the market. Therefore in 2004, in addition to the standard series of cruises with Classic International Cruises' (CIC) *Arion* from Tilbury, no-fly cruises were offered aboard her CIC fleet-mate *Funchal* from Belfast, Dundee,

Greenock, Liverpool, and Newcastle. Departures from Hull and a special cruise from Portsmouth, to commemorate the 200th anniversary of the Battle of Trafalgar, were featured during the following season.

In 2006 it was Louis Cruise Lines' *Calypso* that provided the main CMS cruise programme and in that same year discussions were opened with former colleagues at Transocean about a possible co-operation. By coincidence, the German company had chartered from the same Louis Cruise Lines the 1100 passenger *Aquamarine*, which was to be renamed *Arielle* for the duration of the charter. The British and German cruise markets have different peaks and troughs in demand and it was eventually agreed that CMS would sub-charter

---

MARCO POLO REFURBISHMENT MARCH 2008

During the refurbishment of Marco Polo in March 2008, prior to her introduction into their fleet, Transocean Tours is taking the opportunity to rename her decks and public rooms. Names have been carefully selected to more accurately reflect the vessel's planned itineraries of exploration and discovery that will be undertaken over the next few years and also to achieve a certain uniformity with the style of her Transocean fleetmates, Astor and Astoria.

Consequently the actual names on board Marco Polo will be at variance with those shown in the deck plans produced in earlier editions of the Summer 2008 brochures that are currently in circulation. For easy reference, and to avoid any confusion, a summary of the changes is shown below:

Decks		Public Rooms	
New Name	Former Name	New Name	Former Name
Navigator Deck	Sky Deck	**Marco Polo Lounge**	Ambassador Lounge
Columbus Deck	Upper Deck	**Scott's Bar**	Charleston Club
Amundsen Deck	Promenade Deck	**Captain's Club**	Polo Lounge
Magellan Deck	Belvedere Deck	**Palm Garden**	Palm Court
Pacific Deck	Main Deck	**Columbus Lounge**	Le Bar
Atlantic Deck	Bali Deck	**Marco's**	Raffles
Baltic Deck	Pacific Deck	**Waldorf Restaurant**	Seven Seas Restaurant
Caribic Deck	Safari Deck	**Livingston Lounge**	Library
		Nansen Lounge	Card Room

Transocean Tours
c/o Cruise & Maritime Services International Ltd
274 Main Road
Sutton-at-Hone, Dartford, Kent DA4 9HJ
Tel: 01322 863928; Fax: 0845 430 0274
Email: sales@transoceancruises.co.uk

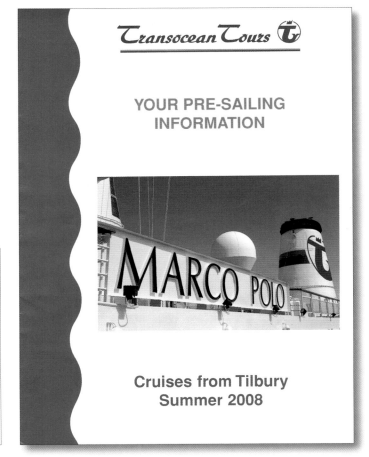

YOUR PRE-SAILING INFORMATION

**Cruises from Tilbury
Summer 2008**

Far left: An information sheet explaining the re-naming of decks and public rooms. (CMV)

Left: Transocean's 2008 Pre Sailing Information leaflet cover. (CMV)

Arielle from Transocean for a short series of cruises in May and June 2007, plus some further sailings in September exclusively for the British market. The other months of the year would be spent with solely German-speaking passengers. Unsurprisingly, Tilbury and Bremerhaven were selected as the respective home ports. As part of the sub-charter arrangement, it was agreed that the UK programme should be marketed under the Transocean Tours' name as this was an internationally established brand, although little known in the United Kingdom.

To the delight, and relief of the Directors, the *Arielle* cruises were a resounding success and sold out very quickly, which made CMS particularly keen to produce and market the 2008 programme. The Dartford premises were extended by the purchase of the neighbouring building and the staff increased to sixteen to deal with the expanding workload. Whilst they were contemplating a second season with *Arielle*, their Transocean counterparts were in fruitful negotiations with the Global Maritime Group about its new acquisition *Marco Polo*, which was to be available for charter from the Spring of 2008. CMS were also keen to re-establish its programme of cruises from UK regional ports which had not operated since 2005 due to the lack of a suitable ship.

Capain Alexander Golubev (CMV)

The outcome of this busy period of talks was that *Marco Polo* would be chartered on a long term basis to Transocean, which in turn, would sub-charter her to CMS for an agreed number of days each year. Therefore in 2008 there would be an exclusive British period from Tilbury between April and August and an exclusive German season from Kiel and Bremerhaven from August with both companies marketing the late autumn and winter 2008-2009 periods which featured the Caribbean, South America and Antarctica. As with the previous season of *Arielle* cruises, *Marco Polo's* 2008 season was marketed under the Transocean Tours banner, giving an important sense of continuity.

A preview brochure was issued covering fourteen cruises that formed the initial UK season. These comprised six Norwegian fjord sailings, three Round British Isles itineraries, plus one cruise each to The North Cape, Iceland, the Baltic Cities & St Petersburg and finally a 'Celtic Explorer' route which sailed anti-clockwise around the British Isles and took in the west coast of Ireland. Such was the demand that a main brochure was never issued and the programme filled on the relatively scanty information contained in the preview edition which had been written in August 2007, long before the new owners took delivery. This meant that much of the ship photography forwarded from Orient Lines as part of the purchase arrangement had to be subtly retouched to take account of the planned Transocean livery. Final decisions had not been taken about the renaming of decks or public rooms and so the eight passenger decks shown in the brochure deck plan still boasted their Orient Lines labels. Similarly, it was not until the first edition of the German brochure for that market's 2008 sailings that the main public rooms were finally re-titled as the now familiar Waldorf Restaurant, Marco Polo Lounge, Captain's Club, Columbus Lounge, Marco's Bistro and Scott's Bar. The new *Marco Polo's* schedule of cruises from the UK was extremely well-received and the ship herself was seen as raising CMS's standards to an entirely new and superior level.

At Transocean's request, the owners appointed a popular Russian captain as their first Master of *Marco Polo*. Captain Alexander Golubyev had served Transocean aboard *Calypso* and *Astor* and held the sought-after designation of 'Ice-Master', as he had cruised Arctic and Antarctic waters more than forty times during his eighteen years' experience. On Saturday 19th April 2008, just twenty seven days after taking delivery of the vessel in Lisbon from NCL / Orient Lines, the first Global Maritime Group cruise sailed from Tilbury with the ship resplendent in her new Transocean livery. CMS had filled the ship with 769 British passengers on a six night 'Springtime Fjordland' itinerary that visited Ulvik and Eidfjord in the Hardangerfjord, then proceeded further north for two calls in the Sognefjord at Vik and Flåm and finally Bergen before returning to Tilbury on Friday 25th April.

Just before she sailed, all passengers were invited to attend an Inaugural Ceremony around the Lido area on Magellan Deck. A typically grey drizzly and windswept April afternoon saw a sizeable audience watch the Transocean House Flag officially being presented to Captain Golubev by Mr Nikolaos Tragakes, Chairman of the Global Maritime Group, who was accompanied by Mr Peter Waehnert, Managing Director of Transocean Tours as well as Chris Coates and Richard Bastow from CMS.

As the first season of cruises proceeded and the inevitable teething problems were ironed out, it seemed that Transocean's emphasis on the ship's 'enviable pedigree...relaxed atmosphere and ... friendly service and customer satisfaction' as well as her 'exquisite' appearance and strong following among British travellers would prove a sound basis for a long and fruitful relationship and they duly announced their intention of operating her until at least 2012.

Transocean's first winter season programme which commenced in Bremerhaven on 6th November 2008, attracted a different type of

passengers who, due to the nature of the itineraries and shore excursions that were on offer, were more 'travellers' than 'tourists'. The ship ran as a dual-language operation with a majority German-speaking passengers. Transocean had a history of producing passengers for a winter programme with their other ships *Astor* and *Astoria*, whilst CMS had never previously offered cruises outside of the main season and consequently had no database of prospective winter passengers. The marketing in the UK had therefore to start from scratch and although the numbers were not huge, English-speaking passengers were well represented on each of the seven cruises which made up this inaugural season. The ship made her way southwards down through the Atlantic on a 25 night 'Voyage to Rio'

At anchor off a Greek island.
(CMV)

49

During the winter of 2008/9, under charter to Transocean Tours, **Marco Polo** offered four Antarctic cruises. (CMV)

Transocean Tours' 2009 brochure. (Mike Tedstone)

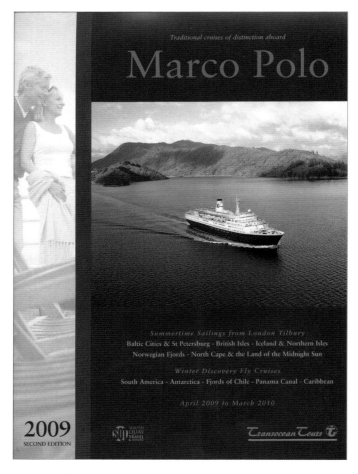

duration Norwegian and Baltic itineraries and their very own 'Around the British Isles' departure from Kiel which finished in Bremerhaven on 5th October.

Unfortunately, a combination of adverse trading and other operational factors combined with poor advanced bookings for the following winter's cruises from Germany resulted in Transocean Tours being forced into provisional administration on 1st September 2009. A sad end for a company that had been trading for 55 years and was much respected internationally. Urgent talks resulted in CMS agreeing to take over the UK charter from 2010 until at least 2015, when the original Transocean charter would have come to an end.

The senior management team at CMS was faced with the considerable challenge of devising and advertising an attractive programme for *Marco Polo*, engaging cruise staff, setting up shore excursion programmes and, most vitally, finding a considerable number of British passengers in the very short period available to them, as well as completing a myriad of other essential tasks. However, since several key members of the team had known the ship since her Soviet days, had worked for CTC and with Transocean over the previous three years, they were in a strong position to analyse the strengths and weaknesses of previous operations. By drawing on the best aspects and avoiding the pitfalls, they were able to put together a new programme which, although familiar in many respects, had a fresh and attractive feel.

and made four Antarctic cruises of varying durations before returning via the Chilean Fjords and the west coast of South America into the Panama Canal and the Caribbean. Crossing the Atlantic via the Azores, she arrived back in Bremerhaven on 8th March 2009.

The shape of the 2009 UK summer programme, which started on 22nd April, was very similar to 2008 with a couple of maiden calls registered in Douglas, Isle of Man, and Seydhisfjordur in Iceland. The last cruise finished in Tilbury on 6th August and Transocean's own season commenced the following day from Bremerhaven. The German passengers were offered differing

Marco Polo's funnel and name board, 31st May 2009 (Ashley Gill)

Sharing the anchorage in Geirangerfjord, Norway with the *Discovery*, 28th May 2009. (Ashley Gill)

A Transocean luggage tag.
(CMV)

A Transocean ticket wallet. (CMV)

Basking in the Norwegian spring sunshine at Rosendal in Hardangerfjord, Norway 30th May 2009. (Ashley Gill)

The basic CMV business model was to offer a range of no-fly, adult-only cruises on board *Marco Polo* from Tilbury and meet the demand for sailings from regional ports that it had been unable to fulfil in previous years due to lack of tonnage. To achieve the latter aim, an additional ship, the *Ocean Countess,* was added to the fleet to operate from the ports of Hull, Liverpool, and Greenock between April and October. With the global recession just beginning to take effect, it may have seemed an inappropriate time for CMV to expand from being a summer season charterer with a single vessel to a full cruise operator with 2 ships and nearly 600 trading days. However, 2009 had seen a dramatic reduction in the levels of competition within the no-fly UK cruise market with *Black Prince*

(Fred Olsen), *Ocean Majesty* (Page & Moy), *Thomson Spirit* (Thomson/TUI) all being withdrawn and some other ships spending more time away from the UK. In addition, the Global Maritime Group also proved hugely supportive through the purchase of a proportion of Messrs. Bastow and Coates' equity in CMV.

The Global Maritime Group was contracted to provide the hotel and passenger services on board *Ocean Countess* in addition to *Marco Polo* which was already fully crewed by them, ensuring that standards were consistent across both ships and providing useful economies of scale. The cruise programme – including the Norwegian Fjords, North Cape, Iceland, Baltic Capitals and Round British voyages –

In the River Thames approaching Tilbury on 1st June 2009. (Ian Boyle, Simplon Postcards)

Marco Polo arriving at London International Cruise Terminal, Tilbury, on 1st June 2009. (Ian Boyle, Simplon Postcards)

would also be broadly similar for both vessels although the location of the various departure ports led to slight variations in the duration and routes of some cruises.

As CMS was marketing a product under its own name for the very first time, Chris Coates devised the tag line 'Britain's newest cruise line' and a more catchy brand name of Cruise & Maritime Voyages (CMV) was introduced. A new logo was developed, which combined the blue and silver typeface and style of Cruise & Maritime Services with a stylistic blue and silver sail which echoed the logo of the Global Maritime Group and represented the strengthening connection between the two companies.

The CMV team's intensive efforts came to fruition on Saturday 2nd January 2010 when *Marco Polo* departed from Tilbury on her inaugural 30 night voyage to The West Indies. This was followed by a return to her old haunts in South America, but this time venturing up the Amazon river as far as Manaus and also to the Orinoco river in Venezuela. The Amazon itinerary has since become an annual event in *Marco Polo's* cruising calendar. Other new ideas for 2010 included trips to view the Northern Lights, the first of which departed in March. Thus, the formula was set and although in subsequent years the programme evolved slightly in the light of experience, with new ports added and others dropped, the philosophy remained unaltered.

With the UK recession in full swing, the 2011 and 2012 cruising

Marco Polo's funnel bearing the new CMV logo.
(Richard Clammer)

Taken on 18th January 2010 during her inaugural CMV cruise to the West Indies, this dramatic photograph shows how the ship's livery sets off her elegant profile to perfection. (CMV)

seasons proved challenging for CMV and during the summer of 2011 a re-structuring took place which saw the Global Maritime Group increase its shareholding while outside investors took positions and brought other businesses into a newly formed group of companies. This action ensured that CMV would remain a significant player in the future UK cruise market. Later in the same year a dedicated sales office was established in the United States with the intention of attracting substantial numbers of North American passengers via the transatlantic gateway airports of London, Edinburgh , Glasgow and Manchester.

Marco Polo operated exclusively out of Tilbury in 2011 and introduced her growing number of repeat passengers to some new

itineraries which included Svalbard (Spitzbergen), Rouen and the River Seine and a December programme to many of Europe's famous Christmas markets.

Her 2012 season was notable for a change of home port during May and June, when she operated four cruises each out Newcastle and Leith to much acclaim. The year of the Royal Diamond Jubilee and the 100th anniversary of the ill-fated *Titanic* maiden voyage provided the opportunity for specially themed sailings. On 10th April she sailed from Tilbury with a group of enthusiasts, including a number booked through the CMV's USA office and visited Cherbourg, Cobh, Belfast and Liverpool on a Maritime Heritage theme which also featured an on board exhibition of original artefacts

Ocean Countess and *Marco Polo* meet in Eidfjord, Norway on 22nd August 2011. (CMV)

from *Titanic* and the White Star liner *Lusitania*. On 28th May an unusual 9-night Diamond Jubilee celebration cruise departed from Leith , visited Belfast, Cardiff and London, the other three capitals of the United Kingdom, as well as Portsmouth, St Mary's in the Isles of Scilly and Douglas in the Isle of Man. While *Marco Polo* continued to maintain her established programme of cruises, the charter of her running mate *Ocean Countess* ended with a final cruise from Liverpool to the Canary Islands which terminated in Barcelona on 22nd October 2012.

In order to ensure the continuation of sailings from UK regional

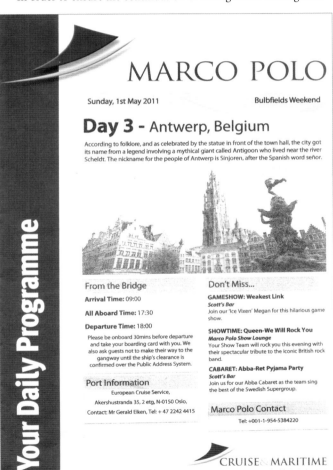

ports, CMV then entered into a unique joint venture arrangement with the All Leisure Group which saw the *Discovery* take *Ocean Countess's* place from April 2013. The same year also saw CMV extend its activities by chartering 600-passenger *Astor* for an initial three winter seasons commencing in 2013, to revive the sailings undertaken by the 'Russian Poets' under charter to CTC back in the 1970s and 80s. Each November the *Astor* sails from Tilbury on a 38 night voyage via the South Atlantic islands, South Africa, Reunion and Mauritius to Fremantle, Australia. Following her arrival, she operates a series of cruises from Fremantle, including a 33 night 'Round Australia' voyage, before returning northbound to the UK during March and April. A CMV Australia office was opened in Sydney to service this new business and to provide Australian passengers with packaged opportunities to cruise in the northern hemisphere on board *Marco Polo*.

Innovations for 2014 included further additions to the on-board programme of complementary activities including guest lecturers, workshops, and entertainers, while three new cruise itineraries were introduced. A D-Day 70th anniversary cruise which left Tilbury on 2nd June visited key locations including Zeebrugge, Portsmouth, Honfleur and Cherbourg, and was enhanced by appropriate shore excursions and on-board lectures. A two week North Cape and Midnight Sun summer cruise which called for the first time at Kirkenes and Murmansk departed on 4th July from Newcastle, while an October sailing from Tilbury took her to a selection of Scandinavian cities and, very appropriately, Wismar where she was launched 50 years ago.

In October 2014 the joint venture arrangement with All Leisure for the operation of *Discovery* by CMV came to close. Portuscale Cruises' *Funchal* took her place for two autumn voyages and it was confirmed that the same company's 550-passenger *Azores* would take over her regional cruise programme in 2015. A month later, on Monday 3rd November 2014, it was also announced on that the 46,052grt, 1250-passenger, *Magellan (ex-Grand Holiday)* would be joining the CMV fleet as their new flagship, operating alongside *Marco Polo, Azores* and *Astor*. Her maiden CMV voyage will be a 12 night cruise sailing from London Tilbury on Sunday 15th March 2015 to Iceland and the Faroes to view the Solar Eclipse and Northern Lights.

Since CMV's inception in 2010 the number of passengers carried has grown from 36,000 a year to a projected 115,000 in

An example of a Daily Programme dated 1st May 2011 when the ship was visiting Antwerp. (CMV)

Having arrived at Antwerp on 1st May 2011, *Marco Polo* takes on fuel from a barge alongside while her passengers enjoy time ashore. This view gives a fine impression of her curved, tiered decks rising above her elegant stern. (Richard Clammer)

On a calm day at Flam, Norway, *Marco Polo* sits above her own reflection. (Fraser Gray)

2015. In addition to its head office at Purfleet, near Tilbury in the UK, CMV now has three additional established international sales office in Fort Lauderdale, Florida, USA, Sydney, Australia and Offenbach in Germany.

A full list of sailings undertaken by *Marco Polo*' during her time with CMV appears later in this book . During these years she has built up a very loyal and enthusiastic following amongst passengers who prefer her intimate scale to that of her larger competitors and such is the volume of repeat bookings that the company set up the 'Columbus Club' to offer enhanced benefits and acknowledge the loyalty of the regular travellers. Exciting plans have been put in place to mark her 50th anniversary season in 2015.

On a rainy 6th June 2012, **Marco Polo** is moored close to the former Royal Yacht **Britannia** in Leith docks, Scotland, prior to sailing on a cruise to St Petersburg and the Baltic Capitals. (Richard Clammer)

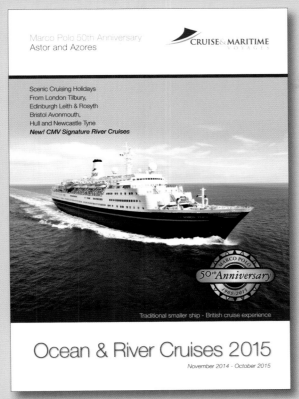

Marco Polo 50th Anniversary
Astor and Azores

CRUISE & MARITIME
VOYAGES

Scenic Cruising Holidays
From London Tilbury,
Edinburgh Leith & Rosyth
Bristol Avonmouth,
Hull and Newcastle Tyne
New! CMV Signature River Cruises

MARCO POLO
50th Anniversary
1965-2015

Traditional smaller ship - British cruise experience

Ocean & River Cruises 2015

November 2014 - October 2015

CMV's 2015 cruise brochure. (CMV)

Discovery in the Bristol Channel outward bound from Avonmouth on 7th September 2014. (Mike Tedstone)

Astor. CMV)

Magellan. (CMV)

Azores. (CMV)

Marco Polo in Eidfjord, Norway,
28th April 2014. (CMV)

MARCO POLO TODAY

So what, exactly, is the charm of this fifty year-old ship? Without doubt her fascinating history, classic good looks, superb sea-keeping qualities and relatively small, 800-passenger capacity are all important factors. In addition the facilities and accommodation on board, so very different to her early days as the *Alexandr Pushkin*, play a major part and are worth examining in some detail.

The majority of the ship's public rooms are located on Magellan Deck (Deck 8). Right forward is the gently-tiered Marco Polo show lounge which is used for the twice-nightly shows put on by the ship's versatile and hard-working entertainments team. These shows generally take place at 2015 and 2215 to fit in with the two meal sittings in the Waldorf restaurant. Different shows are offered each night and are complemented by various speciality acts and guest entertainers. A bar at the forward end of the lounge allows a waiter service for drinks to be offered during performances. The show lounge is also used for lectures during 'sea days' and for mustering passengers for safety briefings. Lifeboat drills are always carried out before the ship leaves her first port and it is re-assuring to see how efficiently these are carried out and, in particular, the thorough way in which any late-comers are chased up and located.

Moving aft one comes to the 'Captain's Club', a restful, full-width lounge with bar and grand piano where musical duos provide an evening programme of light classical music. The muted beige and brown colour scheme, oriental wall panels, deep arm chairs and

Marco Polo at anchor, 28th April 2014. (CMV)

excellent sea views make this a popular spot for quiet relaxation throughout the day. Aft again is the spacious main lobby with reception area to starboard and shore excursions and the future cruise booking desks to port. Moving aft again, the port side has a range of small shops and boutiques, then a conference room often used for day time arts and crafts activities, and the Nansen Card Room, which is adorned with numerous plaques and gifts presented to the ship on her travels and by the *Alexandr Pushkin's* original ship's bell. To starboard is the Palm Garden, a restful seating area with pot plants and wicker chairs and, opposite it, the photographer's display area. Aft again, and mirroring the card room, is the small but delightful Livingstone Library where deep leather chairs provide a comfortable

and quiet haven for the avid reader. Running across the ship, in the space previously occupied by Orient Lines' small casino, is the Columbus Lounge which is a popular gathering place for those eager to watch important events on TV and where duos or individual entertainers often perform during the evenings. Decorated with a large globe and ship's wheel, this pleasant room was designed by Global Maritime Group's naval architect Costas Morfovasilis and its nautical theme blends perfectly with the surrounding spaces.

Doors on both sides of the ship then lead into the full-width Marco's Restaurant which provides self-service, cafeteria-style breakfast, lunch and afternoon tea service and, in the evenings, is transformed into a bistro offering a less formal alternative to the ship's

Contrasts in design at Tallin: This photograph of **Marco Polo** berthed beside the **Grand Mistral** on 11th June 2011 explains why many passengers return again and again to the older, smaller but more elegant ship. (Richard Clammer)

main restaurant. Doors in the glazed after bulkhead lead out onto the timbered open deck, sheltered by the curving promenades above, a bar to starboard and a coffee station/lunchtime grill and pizzeria servery to port. In the centre of this deck is a small swimming pool overlooked by Enzo Plazotta's striking bronze sculpture of Rudolf Nureyev. Depending on local regulations and conditions, the pool is emptied each night, refilled each morning at 0400 and kept immaculately clean.

Above Marco's on Amundsen Deck (Deck 9) is Scott's Bar which is one of the busiest spaces on the ship. During the day time it is used for quizzes, games and afternoon activities, followed by a range of cabarets and other lively entertainments during the evenings. Up another level on Columbus Deck (Deck 10) is the Jade Wellness Centre which provides a gym with all the usual equipment, keep fit classes, and a wide range of massage and other therapies. In the same area are a beauty/hair salon and an internet cafe. Finally, on the aft end of the highest passenger deck, Navigator Deck (Deck10) is a large sunbathing area equipped with sun loungers and three jacuzzis.

The ship's main Waldorf Restaurant occupies the full width of the ship forward on Atlantic Deck (Deck6), a position unchanged since

Marco Polo's current deck plan. (CMV)

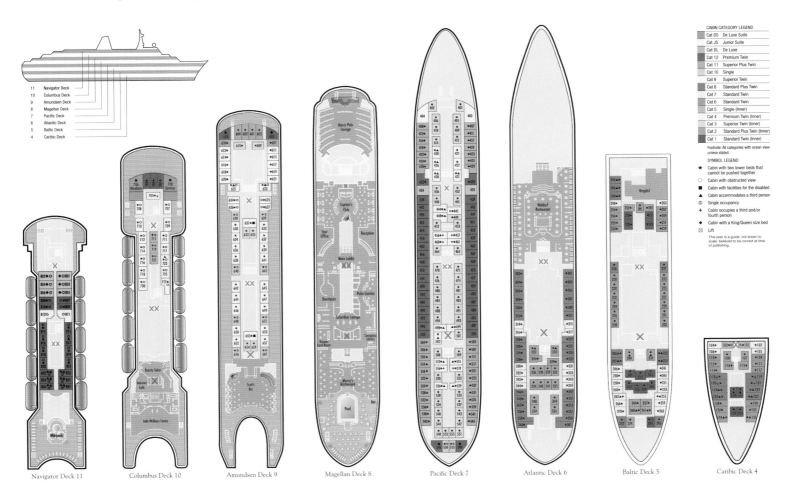

Navigator Deck 11   Columbus Deck 10   Amundsen Deck 9   Magellan Deck 8   Pacific Deck 7   Atlantic Deck 6   Baltic Deck 5   Caribic Deck 4

The Marco Polo Show Lounge. (Richard Clammer)

Alexandr Pushkin's original ship's bell takes pride of place in the Nansen Card room. (Richard Clammer)

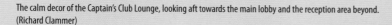

The calm decor of the Captain's Club Lounge, looking aft towards the main lobby and the reception area beyond. (Richard Clammer)

The Nansen Card Room, its walls lined with plaques and trophies presented to the ship during her extensive travels. (Richard Clammer)

The Palm Garden, a quiet seating area on the starboard side of Magellan Deck. (Richard Clammer)

The ship's main lobby and central stairwell, showing some of the oriental art installed during the 1992 refit. (Richard Clammer)

The Livingstone Library, a small but tranquil space with fine sea views. (Richard Clammer)

The Columbus Lounge which joins the port and starboard corridors of Magellan Deck. (Richard Clammer)

The view astern over *Marco Polo's* elegant tiered decks, showing the open air pool, Enzo Plazotta's statue of Rudolf Nureyev and passengers enjoying afternoon tea in the sunshine. (Richard Clammer)

Looking forward from the stern into the curved arms of the ship's terraced outside decks. (Richard Clammer)

Scott's Bar on Amundsen Deck. (Richard Clammer)

The Jade Wellness Centre on Columbus Deck. (John Hendy)

One of the three jacuzzi whirlpools located at the aft end of Navigator Deck are overlooked by a statue of leaping dolphins. (Richard Clammer)

Looking forward along the starboard side of the Waldorf Restaurant on Atlantic Deck, one of the few facilities on the ship still in its original position. (Richard Clammer)

Below: **Marco Polo's** spacious, traditional timber decks are one of her key attractions. This view is looking forward along the port side of Amundsen Deck. (Richard Clammer)

Below right: Looking forward under the port bridge wing towards the spacious forward viewing area on Columbus Deck. (Richard Clammer)

her days as the *Alexandr Pushkin*. There are two sittings, normally at 1830hrs and 2000hrs, the former allowing diners more time to enjoy the full range of evening entertainments and the latter suiting those who prefer to maximise their time on deck at those interesting moments when the ship is leaving port. Service is friendly and efficient, seating at tables of 4,6 or 8, and there is the traditional mix of formal, informal and casual nights.

Marco Polo's open, timber decks are also a major attraction. Unlike some cruise ships it is possible to walk right round the ship, starting at the stern of Amundsen Deck, walking forward beneath the lifeboats in their davits, ascending one level to Columbus Deck , passing round the front of the bridge structure, descending again and returning along the opposite side of the ship. The view forward over the foc's'le from the vast, wonderfully-cambered deck ahead of the curved bridge front is outstanding, while the tiered open decks towards the stern give excellent views over the shapely aft end of Magellan Deck with its pool and iconic Nureyev statue and of the ship's wake stretching out astern.

Accommodation is located in cabins over seven decks. The largest number are to be found on Pacific Deck (Deck 7) which is characterised by its two long corridors which stretch almost the complete length of the ship and reflect her elegant sheer by curving visibly upwards towards the bow and stern. Superior Twin Plus Ocean View cabins are located forward and aft while slightly larger Premium Twin cabins, most of which have two windows, occupy the mid-ships

section. Inboard of the corridors are Premium Twin inner cabins and right forward 4 cabins of 2 different grades overlook the bows.

The three decks below – Atlantic, Baltic and Caribic (Decks 6, 5 & 4)- have a mixture of inside and outside cabins, the latter with portholes rather than windows. Amundsen Deck has just 8 inside cabins, and a similar number of outside cabins for single occupancy, while the majority are Superior Twin Ocean View cabins with windows facing on to the boat deck. Right forward 6 Superior or Premium cabins look overlook the ship's foc's'le. Columbus Deck (Deck 10) has 17 more Superior and Premium grade cabins, 4 inside cabins and the ship's 2 spacious De-Luxe Suites, 'Mandarin' and 'Dynasty'. The topmost Navigator Deck (Deck 11) has more Superior and Premium cabins together with 2 Junior suites.

Perhaps one of the most striking impressions of travelling on board *Marco Polo* is of the friendliness and efficiency of her 336 crew members. Drawn from over 20 different nationalities, the largest contingent is currently from the Ukraine, but Burma, the Philippines, the Indian Sub-Continent, Eastern Europe ,the Baltic states and the UK are all well represented. Bound together by the ship's language of English, they are clearly extremely well trained and hard working, seem to share a very real pride in their ship and are well aware of her unique status within the cruising world. The ship's size also means that passengers recognise and are recognised by a good proportion of the crew, as well as fellow travellers, and are quickly drawn into the ship's friendly atmosphere.

Nightfall at sea as *Marco Polo* leaves the New Waterway en route from Amsterdam to Antwerp, 30th April 2011. (Richard Clammer)

Forward-facing Premium Twin cabin No. 605 on Amundsen Deck. (CMV)

A Premium Twin Ocean View cabin on Pacific Deck. (CMV)

YOUR POCKET SIZE DECK PLAN

CRUISE & MARITIME
VOYAGES

Those crew members seen most often by the passengers are, inevitably, members of the hotel staff. Overseen by the Hotel Manager, this 258-person team is by far the largest on board and is sub-divided into departments with differing areas of responsibility: Housekeeping , Bar, Galley, Restaurant, Entertainment, Guest Services and finally the Purser's Department. In addition to all these, the Hotel Manager is also responsible for the Sanitation Officer, the Inventory Cost Controller and the ship's Printer.

The 53 members of the Housekeeping Department, efficiently marshalled by the Chief Housekeeper, are arguably the ship's unsung heroes. In addition to keeping the public spaces immaculately clean, the large team of cabin stewards and stewardesses are responsible for servicing the cabins, changing towels and bed linen and ensuring that passengers are made welcome and any difficulties or queries dealt with efficiently. They are under particular pressure on turn-round days when all of the cabins have to be cleaned and prepared in the few short hours between the end of one cruise and the start of the next.

Most passengers take for granted the crisp clean tablecloths in the restaurant and the regular changes of bed linen and towels in their cabins, but rarely pause to consider the volume of laundry which a cruise liner generates. On board *Marco Polo* during a typical 14-night cruise no less than 49,000 items of passenger linen are laundered, comprising 21,000 bed sheets, duvets and pillow cases, 22,400 towels and 5,600 bath mats! Add to this 8,540 similar items for the officers and crew; 24,640 tablecloths, napkins and place mats from the restaurants; 1680 crew uniforms plus 420 articles of guest clothing and one can appreciate that the ship's 6 industrial washing machines, 7 dryers and assorted presses are very well used indeed!

Responsibilities for food and beverages fall under the remits of the Executive Chef who runs the galley, the Restaurant Manager and the Bar Manager. Their teams comprise 59 chefs and galley staff, 56 waiters, wine waiters, assistant waiters and buffet attendants and 29 bar staff. The quality of catering is, of course, a critical measure for any cruise ship and the galley staff are kept on their toes ensuring that every menu is appealing and well-cooked and that all individual dietary needs are catered for. The large galley, which is located forward of the Waldorf Restaurant, has separate areas for the preparation of fish, meat, vegetables and soup, as well as an extremely busy bakery which ensures a steady supply of fresh bread and pastries.

The consumption figures for food and beverages on a typical 14 night cruise give pause for thought. Over this period 750 passengers

Under the watchful eye of the Executive Chef, members of the galley staff prepare salads for the next meal. (John Hendy)

The bonded stores where the ship's stocks of alcoholic drinks are kept. (CMV/ Morgan Van Selman)

will consume 1440 kgs of fish, 218 kgs of shellfish and mussels, 5,551 kgs of meat, together with 17,040 kgs of fresh fruit and vegetables. Dairy products include 790 kgs of ice cream, 658 kgs of cheese, 500 kgs of butter and margarine, 4230 litres of milk and 25,000 fresh eggs. In addition, 3088 bottles of wine, 669 bottles of spirits, 4075 cans of beer and 1650 litres of draught beer are consumed, along with 716 litres of fruit juice, 4174 bottles of water and 6887 cans of soft drinks. Add in rice, pasta, flour, spices, cooking oils , 29,976 tea bags and 222kgs of fresh coffee and one has a very substantial fortnightly shopping list!

All this food and drink has to be sourced, pre-ordered and brought on board at various ports, and then stored carefully at precisely the correct temperature and humidity before being prepared, cooked and brought to the table in prime condition. A complex and responsible task for the staff involved.

Another highly-visible team is led by the Cruise Director and is comprised of the 25 entertainers who provide the nightly shows, musicians and performance hosts. This small but busy group is responsible for all entertainments and social activities on board and frequently do more than one job, being seen on stage, helping with passenger embarkation and accompanying shore excursions.

The Guest Services section of the Hotel Department covers the important areas of Reception (which is manned 24 hours a day and has 4 staff) and Shore Excursions where there are normally 2 staff but often 3 on potentially busy cruises such as the Baltic Capitals. There is also a Guest Services host or hostess who looks after the future cruise bookings made on board.

The Purser's Department, headed by the Financial Controller, deals with all cash flow and financial transactions on board including crew wages and passengers' shipboard accounts. Ship clearance procedures at the ports of call and other crewing issues including travel and signing on/off are also part of the role. The I.T. personnel, who maintain the various ship's computer and communication technology systems, fall within this department.

In other areas, there are 3 shop staff , 3 medical personnel, 4 photographers and 4 spa staff all of whom are concessionaires, as well as a varying number of guest lecturers, craft tutors, and visiting personalities all of whom are classed as supernumeraries.

The Deck Department consists of 37 officers and crew who are responsible for the navigation and handling of the ship, maintenance of all outside spaces and deck equipment, and safety issues. They are

The Shore Excursions Desk.
(Richard Clammer)

The boutiques are situated on the port side of Magellan Deck. (Richard Clammer)

led by the Captain, supported by the Staff Captain who is second-in-command and also responsible for all aspects of crew management and training, and the Chief Officer who traditionally acts as the ship's Safety Officer and stands the 0400-0800 and 1600-2000 watches. Below these are the various watch officers, radio and navigation officers and the Bosun overseeing his deck crew.

Passengers enjoying early morning walks on deck will discover the latter hard at work hosing down, sanding deck rails, and maintaining davits and lifeboats. Each day a small area of the deck is discretely closed off while more coats of paint or varnish are applied and quite frequently, after sailing from a port of call, the fo'c'sle crew will be seen with white paint and rollers to touch up all the fairleads, rollers and capstans which had been even slightly marked by rope handling!

The bridge with its adjoining chart room and communications

At 0500 on a sunny morning, members of the deck crew are already hard at work on cleaning and continuous maintenance as the ship approaches Stockholm on 15th June 2012. (Richard Clammer)

office is a fascinating period piece. Too late for brass telegraphs and fittings and too early for today's fully-computerised appearance, it is characterised by robust metal consoles, large dials and mechanical switches. Within the wonderfully 1960s setting, however, every modern, electronic navigational aid is present and in full use by the ship's officers.

Set back from the front of the bridge, a long console with slightly angled ends runs athwartships. In the centre, as one would expect, is the ship's wheel, autopilot, joy stick controls, giro compass and helm indicators, flanked by various radios and banks of switches. On the deck head above is a gyro repeater and a prismatic device through which it is possible for the helmsman to read the magnetic compass on the compass platform above. Set beneath the central wheelhouse window is a traditional magnetic bowl compass with prismatic sights with which visual bearings can be taken.

On the main console to port are electronic chart plotter and radar screens and banks of switches, while to starboard are the engine room telegraphs, stabilizer controls, various VHF and other radios, depth sounder readout, three more radar or chart plotter screens, internal telephones and the Captain's large leather chair. A live CCTV feed enables the master to view the full length of the ship to both port and starboard from this position.

On each of the open bridge wings is a large weatherproof stainless steel cabinet containing duplicate telegraphs, steering joy sticks and other controls, to enable the master to manoeuvre the ship effectively while entering or leaving port and a raised wooden grating to improve his line of sight. Bolted to the inside of each bridge wing is a brass and mahogany plaque reminding him that, from that position, there is precisely 52 m of ship ahead of him and 124m astern!

Behind the wheelhouse on the port side is the chartroom where, reassuringly, paper charts are in constant use by the navigators as a back-up to the modern electronic systems. Beneath the two full-sized chart tables are drawers for storing charts, while the walls are lined with notice boards and bookcases containing many of the safety and guidance files which are required by passenger ships today. Adjoining the chart room is the communications office/ radio room, equipped with an impressive array of VHF and other radios, NAVTEX, text, internet and satellite communications equipment.

Adjoining the wheelhouse to starboard are the Captain's quarters. In addition to his sleeping quarters, he has a spacious day cabin which combines the role of relaxation area and office. Welcoming sofas and

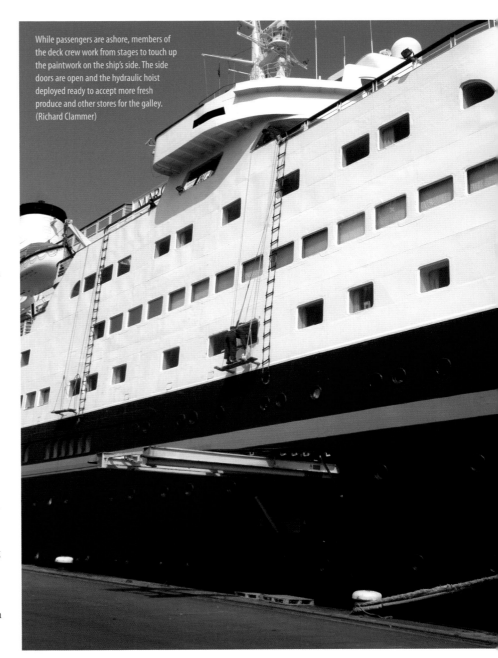

While passengers are ashore, members of the deck crew work from stages to touch up the paintwork on the ship's side. The side doors are open and the hydraulic hoist deployed ready to accept more fresh produce and other stores for the galley. (Richard Clammer)

Mooring ropes are already flaked out on the foredeck as the ship approaches her berth at Warnemunde, Germany, on 9th June 2012. Close inspection reveals the anchor cables and capstans, rope storage bins, the hydraulic cranes and the short mast which supports the forward navigation lights. (Richard Clammer)

easy chairs are there to enjoy during rare off-duty moments, but the rest of space is given up to a large desk, flanked by bookcases containing numerous files of paperwork. From here he deals with staff training, safety management, passage and schedule planning, and many other aspects of his complex and demanding role. All these are, of course, in addition to actually navigating and handling the ship at sea!

The Chief Engineer leads a department of 33 technical staff who, in addition to the propulsion machinery, are also responsible for all of the electrical, plumbing and heating systems on board. All maintenance is computerised and carried out to a carefully-planned

schedule and, during any particular voyage, at least one piece of equipment, such as a generator set, will be undergoing a full service. The company's Greek-based Superintendent Engineer is frequently on board to support the Chief with planned maintenance . Major and underwater work is carried out during the ship's annual dry docking which usually takes place in November.

The engine room is a revelation in itself: a cavernous space rising the entire height of the ship, in which the main engines, their various feed pipes and parts colour-coded and painted in a most unusual and attractive manner, stand in state. Around them are grouped the various

Capt. Georgios Antonellos (right) and watch keepers on *Marco Polo's* bridge, 10th June 2012. (Richard Clammer)

Capt. Nikolaos Michaloliakos stands on the starboard bridge wing next to the compass platform and the duplicate controls which are used when docking. (John Hendy)

auxiliaries, maintenance workshops, and other essential facilities.

A remarkable fact about *Marco Polo* is that she is still powered by her original, 1965 main engines which are still working faultlessly. These are a pair of heavy, 2-stroke,7-cylinder, 21,000 H.P. crosshead model SultzerRD76 diesels with a 76 cm cylinder bore, which are capable of running on a variety of fuels from light diesel to heavy (600CST) fuel oil. At an average cruising speed of 16 knots they run at 120 R.P.M. while at full speed (19.5 knots) they consume 3,300 kg of fuel per hour. Their Sulzer patent oil pumps will run for 100,000 hours between services and the experienced Chief Engineer, Georgios Katsifarakis, insists that, based on his long experience of working with different models of Sulzer engine, the *Marco Polo's* are by far the most reliable type –'simple, strong and easy going'. The engines drive 2, 4-bladed bronze propellers, each 8½ meters in diameter.

Engine orders come by telegraph from the bridge to a glazed control room which, with large, robust instruments in the same style as those on the bridge, is another splendid example of 1960s design. The only modern feature, on the starboard side of the control room, is a bank of controls for the ship's 4, 6-cylinder Wartsila diesel generators which were installed during 2009. Each has an output of 1,200 KW, giving a total of 4,800KW on full power, but any 2 can provide the ship's full power requirements, including the single 1197 BHP bow thruster, extendable fin stabilizers, deck and boat-handling equipment, refrigeration and cold storage, air conditioning, lighting and domestic power circuits.

The ship is also fitted with an osmosis fresh water plant capable of producing about 17 tons per hour (this varies slightly with the salinity of the incoming seawater) meeting the ship's average consumption of 260-300 tons per day and making her fully self-sufficient during long ocean crossings.

Chief Engineer Katsifarakis is a huge enthusiast for his ship, describing her as 'the last Rolls Royce from the golden era of travelling at sea' and is justifiably proud of his spotlessly clean and meticulously maintained domain.

During her time with Cruise & Maritime Voyages, successive captains have enthused about the ship and her sea-keeping and handling qualities. Her deep draft and low freeboard make her far less prone to windage whilst manoeuvring in close quarters than large , modern cruise ships, while her powerful, ice-strengthened bows and kindly hull shape, designed to withstand the rigours of the North Atlantic, make for a relatively comfortable ride even in the heaviest of

A navigating officer at work in the chartroom. (Richard Clammer)

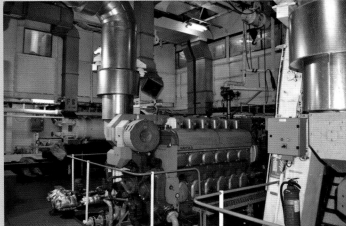

Opposite page: *Marco Polo's* cavernous and immaculate engine room, showing her two original and brightly-painted Sulzer engines. Chief Engineer Georgios Katsifarakis stands on the upper walkway. (John Hendy)

One of the four Wartsila generators which provide the ship's electrical power. (John Hendy)

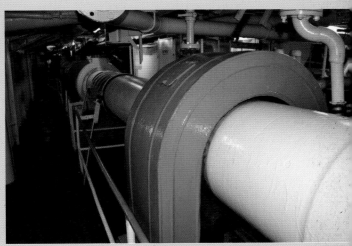

One of the two propeller shafts. The red and yellow objects in the distance are brakes and bearings respectively. (CMV/Morgan Van Selman)

The scarlet-painted builder's plate and engine room bell. (John Hendy)

Inside the soundproofed engine control room. The coloured levers are the ahead/astern controls and the throttles for each of the main engines. (Richard Clammer)

Global Maritime Group's office in Athens, Greece. A highly skilled and professional team of over 40 staff look after crewing (including worldwide travel arrangements), all aspects of deck, engine room, technical, hotel and entertainment management and all marine matters including port agency, bunkering and ship's supplies. Quite an amazing operation.

26th April 2014 marked the Golden Anniversary of *Marco Polo's* launch and 2015 will be her 50th season in service. A number of special events have been planned to mark this significant milestone in her life. Chief amongst these is a special 36 night commemorative cruise from Tilbury to Canada during which she will revisit Quebec and Montreal, the destinations on her maiden transatlantic crossing, and a number of other ports where she was a familiar sight during her Soviet cruises from Montreal. Having departed from the Thames on Friday 24th July, she will call at Lerwick (Shetlands), Tórshavn (Faroes) and Reykjavik (Iceland) before visiting three ports in Greenland. She will then proceed to St John's (Newfoundland), Sydney (Nova Scotia), Charlottetown (Prince Edward Island), Gaspé, and up the St Lawrence River to Quebec and Montreal. After some lively celebrations she departs again for Saguenay, Sept îsles, Havre-Saint -Pierre, Cap-aux-Meules (îsles de la Madelaine, Corner Brook (Newfoundland) and L'Anse aux Meadows (Newfoundland) before re-crossing the Atlantic to Cobh (Ireland) and Tilbury. The cruise was fully booked almost as soon as it was advertised, leading to the provision of a second 34 night autumn commemorative voyage from Tilbury via Cherbourg to Canada, but omitting Greenland due to the predicted local ice conditions. The voyage will include overnight stays at Quebec and Montreal and a call at Halifax, Nova Scotia, before returning to the UK via Cobh.

weather. Most have admitted to a delight in handling her, and believe that *Marco Polo* is an ideally sized ship, large enough to undertake long ocean crossings in comfort but small enough to reach ports which are inaccessible to larger vessels, and also of a size where a real sense of community can be built up among the crew and passengers.

Rather unusually, the management of the ship's entire operation (together with that of her fleet mates) is handled in-house by the

The remainder of her Golden Anniversary season will be filled with her usual selection of Round Britain sailings, cruises to the

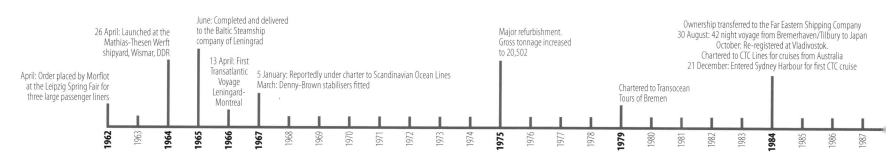

April: Order placed by Morflot at the Leipzig Spring Fair for three large passenger liners

26 April: Launched at the Mathias-Thesen Werft shipyard, Wismar, DDR

June: Completed and delivered to the Baltic Steamship company of Leningrad

13 April: First Transatlantic Voyage Leningard-Montreal

5 January: Reportedly under charter to Scandinavian Ocean Lines
March: Denny-Brown stabilisers fitted

Major refurbishment. Gross tonnage increased to 20,502

Chartered to Transocean Tours of Bremen

Ownership transferred to the Far Eastern Shipping Company
30 August: 42 night voyage from Bremerhaven/Tilbury to Japan
October: Re-registered at Vladivostok.
Chartered to CTC Lines for cruises from Australia
21 December: Entered Sydney Harbour for first CTC cruise

1962 1963 1964 1965 1966 1967 1968 1969 1970 1971 1972 1973 1974 1975 1976 1977 1978 1979 1980 1981 1982 1983 1984 1985 1986 1987

Norwegian fjords, Iceland, the Baltic Cities and St Petersburg, visits to north west European ports and a number of events alongside at Tilbury. In addition she will undertake the now-traditional 42-night January departure via Amsterdam, Portugal, Madeira and the Cape Verdes to Brazil and the Amazon. After visiting four locations on the mighty river, she calls at the infamous Devil's Island in French Guiana, then the Caribbean islands of Grenada, St.Vincent, the Grenadines, St. Lucia and Barbados before crossing back to the Azores and the UK.

All of these cruises are expected to be more than usually filled with repeat bookings from admirers of this remarkable ship which, as a result of her initial design and strong construction, her extensive 1990s refit and meticulous maintenance and improvement ever since, is sailing proudly into her 50th year. Having already sailed hundreds of thousands of miles around the globe, *Marco Polo* should continue to sail for many more, attracting the admiring gaze of all who see her and the affection of those lucky enough to travel onboard. Truly a stunning survivor from the great age of ocean liners.

Illuminated after dark, *Marco Polo* makes a welcoming sight. (CMV)

6 February: Laid up in Singapore and put up for sale by Morflot

8 July: Sold to Shipping & General Ltd.for operation by Orient Lines Renamed Marco Polo and re-registered at Nassau, Bahamas 1991-93: Major re-build in Greece

19 November: Marco Polo's maiden voyage, Mombasa to Cape Town

Orient Line and Marco Polo sold to Norwegian Cruise Lines

1 September: Transocean Tours goes into Provisional Administration September: Cruise & Maritime agrees to take over the charter from Global Maritime Group

23 March: Vessel delivered to Global in Lisbon 19 April: Maiden Transocean Cruise from Tilbury

4 June: Sale announced to the Global Maritime Group, who charter her to Transocean Tours

2 January: Maiden CMV Cruise sailed from Tilbury

10 April: Undertook special Maritime Heritage Cruise to commemorate the Titanic centenary

2nd June: D-Day Anniversary Cruise

24 July: 50th Anniversary commemorative voyage to Canada & Greenland

1990 1991 1992 **1993** 1994 1995 1996 1997 **1998** 1999 2000 2001 2002 2003 2004 2005 2006 **2007** **2008** **2009** **2010** 2011 **2012** 2013 **2014** **2015**

ACKNOWLEDGEMENTS & REFERENCES

The author wishes to extend his sincere thanks to all those who have helped with the preparation of this book. Its completion has only been possible because of the generosity of the many individuals and institutions who have been willing to share their specialist knowledge of *Marco Polo's* history, allow access to their archives and photographic collections, and provide valued advice and assistance.

Richard Bastow, Meriel Lowe and David Trevor- Jones were all central to the project, sharing their extensive knowledge of the ship, allowing access to their archives and photographic collections and proof reading the manuscript. Capt. Benjamin De Haas, Camilla Nissen Kerrn of naval architects Knut E. Hansen A/S, and David Yellow provided details of *Marco Polo's* 1991-93 rebuild.

Ian Boyle kindly allowed free access to his extensive collection of photographs of 'The Russian Poets' which appear on his superb and informative website Simplon Postcards, and put me in touch with a number of other key people. John & Myra Allen, Tony Boemi (Vice President, Growth & Development, of the Montreal Port Authority) Christian Bricchi, Andrew Cooke, Ashley Gill, Fotoflite, Fraser Grey, John Hendy, Darren Holdaway, Nevin Jerkovic, Peter Knego, Ken Larwood, John Mavin, Mike Penny, William Mayes, Peter Newell, Bruce Peter, Peter Plowman, Mike Tedstone and Mehemet Yapici of www.fotio.com all kindly provided photographs, material or advice.

At Cruise & Maritime Voyages Commercial Director Chris Coates, Head of Marketing Mike Hall, and designers Ryan Jackson and Alan Zini have all given much support. Thanks are also due to Capt. Pino Sumbula and Voula Karnezi of Global Maritime's Marine Department.

On board *Marco Polo* herself Capt. Nikolas Michaloliakos and former Capt Georgios Antonellos, Chief Engineer Georgios Katsifarakis, Hotel Director Daniel Reiter, former Passenger Services Director Morgan Van Selman, Sheena Allsopp and other members of the crew showed great patience and courtesy in answering my many enquiries.

Miles Cowsill and Clare Price of Ferry Publications, together with designer Ian Smith saw the book smoothly through the publication process.

Finally, my wife Carol demonstrated her customary patience and good humour throughout the project and spent many hours proof reading and editing.

Books and articles

Clammer, Richard, 'Marco Polo' in *Ferry & Cruise Ship Annual 2013,* Ferry Publications, 2013

Dawson, Philip, *The Liner: Retrospective & Renaissance,* W.W. Norton & Co., New York, 2006 & Conway Maritime Press, 2007

Kludas, Arnold., *Great Passenger Ships of the World Today,* Patrick Stephens Ltd, 1992

Miller, William H., *The Cruise Ships,* Conway Maritime Press, 1988

Miller, William H.,*Pictorial Encyclopaedia of Ocean Liners, 186-1994,* Dover Publications, 1994

Miller, William H., *Transatlantic Liners 1945-1980,* Arco Publishers, 1981

Peter, Bruce, *75 years of Ship Design,* Ferry Publications, 2012

Plowman, Peter, *Australian Cruise Ships,* Rosenburg Publishing, 2007

Ponsford, Capt. S. J., *Report of the Preliminary Inquiry into the grounding and foundering of Mikhail Lermontov,* New Zealand Ministry of Transport, February 1986.

Robinson, Murray, 'The Sinking of the Mikhail Lermontov' in *Sea Breezes,* July 2011.

Trevor-Jones, David, 'Soviet Russia's 'Author class" in *Ferry & Cruise Ship Annual 2010,* Ferry Publications, 2010.

Wilson, E.A., *Soviet Passenger Ships 1917-1977,*World Ship Society, 1978

Young, Gavin, *Slow Boats Home,* Hutchinson 1985 & Penguin Books 1986

Websites

www.simplonpc.co.uk A superb, comprehensive site with photo galleries and histories of ocean liners, cruise ships, ferries, excursion ships, UK historic ships, ports, piers and more.

www.ssmaritimecom An Australian website run by shipping enthusiast Reuben Goossens.

www.sealetter.com The Sealetter Cruise Magazine

www.castlesofthe seas.nl

www.cruisecritic.co.uk

www.cruisebusiness.com

www.photoio.com

Marco Polo anchored off the dramatic volcanic coastline of Heimaey with Mt Eyjafjallajokull in the background, 29th June 2011. (John Allen)

MARCO POLO: TECHNICAL INFORMATION

Builders:	V.E.B. Mathias Thesen Werft, Wismar, former East Germany.
Launched:	26th April 1964
Delivered:	14th August 1965
Original Name:	Alexandr Pushkin (1964-1991)
Converted:	1991-93
Flag:	Bahamas
Port of Registry:	Nassau
Owners & Managers:	The Global Maritime Group
Operators:	Cruise & Maritime Voyages
Call Sign:	C6JZ7
Official Number:	716438
IMO Number:	6417097
MMSI Number:	308693000
Classification:	Det Norske Veritas +A1 Passenger Ship ICE -1C
Length overall:	176.29m (578.35ft)
Length between perpendiculars:	155.00m. (508.6ft)
Beam:	23.63m (77.26ft)
Draught:	8.62m (28.3 ft)
Air Draught (Height above the waterline):	48.05m (157.7 ft)

Gross Tonnage:	22,080
Net tonnage:	9,801
Deadweight:	6,472
Decks:	12
Machinery:	2 x 7-cylinder 21,000BHP SulzerRD76 crosshead diesel engines (76cm bore) driving 2 four-bladed bronze propellers, each 8½ meters in diameter.
Speed:	19.5 knots maximum, 15.5 knots cruising speed.
Fuel consumption:	3,300 kg / hour at full speed.
Electrical power:	4 x 6-cylinder Wartsila diesel generators (installed 2009, each with an output of 1,200 KW, giving a total of 4,800KW on full power.
Auxiliary machinery:	Bow thruster, two retractable fin stabilizers, osmosis fresh water plant
Passengers:	800 in 425 cabins (max 900)
Crew:	325-360
Ship's tenders:	4 (2x100 persons, 2 x 70 persons) Total 340 persons
Life boats:	Partially enclosed type for 960 persons
Liferafts:	Launching type, total capacity 625 persons

MARCO POLO'S MASTERS & CHIEF ENGINEERS UNDER GLOBAL MARITIME GROUP OWNERSHIP

MASTERS:

Capt. Alexandr Golubyev	2008
Capt. Sergiy Zhygalin	2008
Capt. Georgios Antonellos	2008 – 2012
Capt. Konstantinos Gritzelis	2008 – 2009
Capt. Matco Antisic	2009 – 2010
Capt. Valentyn Zhukov	2009 – present
Capt. Emmanouil Psarrakis	2013 – present
Capt. Nektarios Rigas	2013 – 2014
Capt. Nikolaos Michaloliakos	2014 – present

CHIEF ENGINEERS:

Viktor Novodon	2008 – 2009
Alexandr Sedchenko	2008 – 2011
Dragan Djuraskovic	2009 – 2010
Sergiy Karpushev	2011 – 2013
Georgios Katsifarakis	2011 – present
Dimitrios Belekos	2014

Capt. Valentyn Zhukov is *Marco Polo's* current senior master. (CMV)

Sailing Date	From	Nights	Ports of Call
19 April 2008	Tilbury	6	Ulvik, Eidfjord, Vik, Flåm, Bergen.
25 April 2008	Tilbury	6	Ulvik, Eidfjord, Vik, Flåm, Bergen.
01 May 2008	Tilbury	6	Ulvik, Eidfjord, Vik, Flåm, Bergen.
07 May 2008	Tilbury	9	Invergordon, Kirkwall, Portree, Tobermory, Dublin, St. Mary's, St. Peter Port.
16 May 2008	Tilbury	6	Ulvik, Eidfjord, Vik, Flåm, Bergen.
22 May 2008	Tilbury	8	Bergen, Molde, Åndalsnes, Geiranger, Vik, Flåm, Eidford.
30 May 2008	Tilbury	7	Ulvik, Eidfjord, Flåm, Hellesylt, Geiranger, Bergen.
06 June 2008	Tilbury	9	Invergordon, Kirkwall, Stornoway, Tobermory, Dublin, St. Mary's, St. Peter Port.
15 June 2008	Tilbury	12	Ulvik, Eidfjord, Olden, Gravdal, Svolvaer, Hammerfest, Honningsvåg, Tromso, Svartisen Glacier, Alesund, Bergen.
27 June 2008	Tilbury	12	Kirkwall, Heimaey, Reykjavik, Grundarfjord, Akureyri, Tórshavn, Lerwick.
09 July 2008	Tilbury	9	Invergordon, Kirkwall, Portree, Tobermory, Dublin, St. Mary's, St. Peter Port.
18 July 2008	Tilbury	12	Kiel Canal, Warnemünde, Tallinn, St. Petersburg, Helsinki, Stockholm, Copenhagen, Kiel Canal.
30 July 2008	Tilbury	11	Honfleur, St Helier, Cobh, Glengariff, Killybegs, Belfast, Stornoway, Kirkwall, Leith.
10 August 2008	Tilbury	1	Bremerhaven.
11 August 2008	Bremerhaven	7	Geiranger, Balestrand, Fjaerland, Bergen, Oslo, Copenhagen, Kiel.
18 August 2008	Kiel	7	Tallinn, St. Petersburg, Helsinki, Stockholm.
25 August 2008	Kiel	11	Copenhagen, Riga, St. Petersburg, Helsinki, Tallinn, Stockholm.
05 September 2008	Kiel	4	Copenhagen, Oslo, Heligoland, Bremerhaven.
09 September 2008	Bremerhaven	12	Rosyth, Invergordon, Stornoway, Belfast, Killybegs, Glengariff, Cobh, Falmouth, Dover.
21 September 2008	Bremerhaven	6	Flåm, Gudvangen, Hellesylt, Geiranger, Bergen.
27 September 2008	Bremerhaven	6	Le Havre, Dover, Zeebrugge, Ijmuiden.
03 October 2008	Bremerhaven	34	Tilbury, Ponta Delgada, St. John's, Philipsburg, Gustavia, Road Town, Basseterre, Castries, Bridgetown, Kingstown, Bequia, Mayreau, St. Georges, Scarborough, Fort de France, Funchal, Lisbon, Tilbury.
06 November 2008	Bremerhaven	23	Lisbon, Funchal, Mindelo. Praia, Belém, Fortaleza, Natal, Recife, Salvador, Rio de Janeiro.
29 November 2008	Rio de Janeiro	18	Montevideo, Buenos Aires, Puerto Madryn, PortStanley, West Point, Elephant Is, Hope Bay, Deception Is, Cape Horn, Puerto Williams, Ushuaia.
17 December 2008	Ushuaia	12	Port Stanley, West Point, Elephant Is, Hope Bay, Deception Is, Cape Horn, Puerto Williams.
28 December 2008	Ushuaia	13	Puerto Williams, Cape Horn, Elephant Is, Hope Bay, Paradise Bay, King George Is, Deception Is, Port Stanley, West Point.
10 January 2009	Ushuaia	14	Paradise Bay, Hope Bay, King George Island, Cape Horn, Puerto Williams, Ushuaia, Punta Arenas, Puerto Montt, Valparaiso.
24 January 2009	Valparaiso	19	Antofagasta, Arica, Callao, Guayaquil, Manta, Transit Panama Canal, San Blas Is. Puerto Limon, Isla San Andres, Kingston, Santo Domingo.
12 February 2009	Santo Domingo	24	St. John's, Road Town, Philipsburg, Pointe a Pitre, Fort de France, Bridgetown, St. Georges, Mayreau, Ponta Delgada, Funchal, Lisbon, Dover, Bremerhaven.
08 March 2009	Bremerhaven		**Final arrival of the 2009 winter season.**
			DOCKING PERIOD
22April 2009	Tilbury	6	Ulvik, Eidfjord, Gudvangen, Flåm, Bergen.
28April 2009	Tilbury	7	Ulvik, Eidfjord, Flåm, Geiranger, Bergen.
05 May 2009	Tilbury	8	Invergordon, Portree, Douglas, Dublin, St. Peter Port, Honfleur.
13 May 2009	Tilbury	11	Copenhagen, Warnemünde, Tallinn, St. Petersburg, Helsinki, Stockholm, Kiel Canal.
24 May 2009	Tilbury	8	Bergen, Molde, Åndalsnes, Geiranger, Flåm, Vik, Rosendal.
01 June 2009	Tilbury	9	Invergordon, Stornoway, Tobermory Dublin, St Mary's, St. Peter Port, Honfleur.
10 June 2009	Tilbury	12	Rosendal, Nordfjordeid, Olden, Gravdal, Svolvaer, Hammerfest, Honningsvåg, Tromso, Svartisen Glacier, Alesund, Bergen.
22 June 2009	Tilbury	12	Kirkwall, Heimaey, Reykjavik, Isafjordur, Akureyri, Seydisfjordur, Tórshavn, Lerwick.
04 July 2009	Tilbury	10	Invergordon – Cruise terminated and vessel returned to Tilbury.
14 July 2009	Tilbury	12	Kiel Canal, Warnemünde, Tallinn, St. Petersburg, Helsinki, Stockholm, Copenhagen, Kiel Canal.
26 July 2009	Tilbury	11	Honfleur, St Helier, Cobh, Glengariff, Killybegs, Belfast, Portree, Kirkwall, Rosyth.
06 August 2009	Tilbury	1	Bremerhaven.
07 August 2009	Bremerhaven	13	Flåm, Alesund, Molde, Trondheim, Honningsvåg, Tromso, Leknes, Svartisen Glacier, Geiranger, Hellesylt, Bergen, Kiel.
20 August 2009	Kiel	11	Copenhagen, Riga, St. Petersburg, Helsinki, Tallinn, Stockholm.

31 August 2009	Kiel	7	Flåm, Gudvangen, Hellesylt, Geiranger, Bergen, Oslo, Copenhagen.
07 September 2009	Kiel	7	Tallinn, St. Petersburg, Helsinki, Stockholm.
14 September2009	Kiel	7	Flåm, Gudvangen, Hellesylt, Geiranger, Bergen, Oslo, Copenhagen.
21 September2009	Kiel	14	Bergen, Lerwick, Invergordon, Stornoway, Belfast, Killybegs, Glengariff, Cobh, St Mary's, Southampton, Dover, Bremerhaven.
05 October 2009	Bremerhaven	34	Tilbury, Plymouth, Ponta Delgada, St. John's, Philipsburg, Road Town, Basseterre, Castries, Bridgetown, Kingstown, Bequia, Mayreau, St. Georges, Scarborough, Fort de France, Funchal, Lisbon, Plymouth, Tilbury.
08 November 2009	Bremerhaven		**Final arrival of 2009 season.**

LAY – UP PERIOD

02 January 2010	Tilbury	30	Amsterdam, Ponta Delgada, St. John's, Philipsburg, Gustavia, Basseterre, Bridgetown, Kingstown, Bequia, Castries, Funchal, Lisbon.
01 February 2010	Tilbury	42	Amsterdam, Lisbon, Tenerife, Mindelo, Belém, Almeirim, Alto do Chao, Parintins, Manaus, Boca da Valéria, Santarem, Paraiso, MacapáÎle du Salut, Puerto Ordaz, Scarborough, Bridgetown, Ponta Delgada.
15 March 2010	Tilbury	14	Amsterdam, Molde, Svartisen Glacier, Svolvaer, Narvik, Tromso, Alta, Alesund, Bergen.
29 March 2010	Tilbury	14	Vigo, Agadir, Arrecife, Tenerife, La Gomera, Funchal, Leixoes.
12 April 2010	Tilbury	11	Cherbourg, Vigo, Lisbon, Cadiz, Gibraltar, Tangier, Portimao. Gijón.
23 April 2010	Tilbury	6	Rouen, St Peter Port, St Mary's.
29 April 2010	Tilbury	3	Amsterdam, Antwerp.
02 May 2010	Tilbury	6	Ulvik, Eidfjord, Vik, Flåm, Bergen.
08 May 2010	Tilbury	9	Invergordon, Stornoway, Tobermory Dublin, St Mary's, St. Peter Port, Honfleur.
17 May 2010	Tilbury	7	Ulvik, Eidfjord, Skjolden, Hellesylt, Geiranger, Bergen.
24 May 2010	Tilbury	8	Bergen, Molde, Åndalsnes, Geiranger, Flåm, Vik, Eidfjord.
01 June 2010	Tilbury	9	Invergordon, Stornoway, Tobermory Dublin, St Mary's, St. Peter Port, Honfleur.
10 June 2010	Tilbury	12	Ulvik, Eidfjord, Olden, Leknes, Hammerfest, Honningsvåg, Tromso, Svartisen Glacier, Alesund, Bergen
22 June 2010	Tilbury	12	Kirkwall, Heimaey, Reykjavik, Isafjordur, Akureyri, Seydisfjordur, Tórshavn, Lerwick.
04 July 2010	Tilbury	11	Invergordon, Kirkwall, Stornoway, Tobermory Dublin, Holyhead, St Mary's, St. Peter Port, Honfleur.
15 July 2010	Tilbury	15	Lerwick, Geiranger, Svartisen Glacier, Honningsvåg, Longyearbyen, Magdalenafjord, NyAlesund, Tórshavn, Stornoway.
30 July 2010	Tilbury	12	Kiel Canal, Warnemünde, Tallinn, St. Petersburg, Helsinki, Stockholm, Kalundborg, Kiel Canal.
11 August 2010	Tilbury	8	Bergen, Molde, Åndalsnes, Geiranger, Flåm, Vik, Eidfjord.
19 August 2010	Tilbury	10	Leith, Bergen, Hellesylt, Geiranger, Olden, Flåm, Vik, Lerwick.
29 August 2010	Tilbury	10	Cherbourg, St Mary's, Glengariff, Killybegs, Belfast, Peel, Portree, Invergordon.
08 September2010	Tilbury	12	Oslo, Kalundborg, Tallinn, St. Petersburg, Helsinki, Stockholm, Kiel Canal.
20 September 2010	Tilbury	14	Gijón, Portimao, Gibraltar, Tangier, Port Mahon, Palma, Ibiza, Lisbon.
04 October 2010	Tilbury	12	Copenhagen, Warnemünde, Tallinn, St. Petersburg, Helsinki, Nynashamn, Kiel Canal.
16 October2010	Tilbury	14	Vigo, Agadir, Arrecife, Tenerife, Funchal, Leixoes.
30 October 2010	Tilbury		**Final arrival of the 2010 season.**

DOCKING PERIOD

03 December 2010	Tilbury	3	Amsterdam, Zeebrugge.
6 December 2010	Tilbury	35	Amsterdam, Ponta Delgada, St. John's, Basseterre, Castries, Soufriere, Kralendijk, Willemstad, Oranjestad St. Georges, Kingstown, Bequia Bridgetown, Funchal, Lisbon.
10 January 2011	Tilbury	42	Amsterdam, Lisbon, Tenerife, Mindelo, Icoaraci, Almeirim, Alto do Chao, Santarem, Parintins, Manaus, Boca da Valéria, MacapáÎle du Salut, Scarborough, Castries, Bridgetown, Ponta Delgada.
21 February 2011	Tilbury	14	Amsterdam, Molde, Svartisen Glacier, Bodo, Narvik, Tromso, Alta, Tromso.
07 March 2011	Tilbury	14	Amsterdam, Alesund, Svartisen Glacier, Svolvaer, Narvik, Tromso, Alta, Molde, Bergen.
21 March 2011	Tilbury	14	Amsterdam, Molde, Svartisen Glacier, Svolvaer, Narvik, Tromso, Alta, Alesund, Bergen.
04 April 2011	Tilbury	2	Amsterdam.
06 April 2011	Tilbury	9	Invergordon, Stornoway, Tobermory Dublin, St Mary's, St. Peter Port, Honfleur.
15 April 2011	Tilbury	8	Oslo, Helsingborg, Copenhagen, Warnemünde, Kiel Canal, Amsterdam.
23 April 2011	Tilbury	6	St Mary's, St Peter Port, Rouen.

MARCO POLO CRUISES APRIL 2008 TO DECEMBER 2014

29 April 2011	Tilbury	3	Amsterdam, Antwerp.
02 May 2011	Tilbury	6	Ulvik, Eidfjord, Flåm, Gudvangen, Bergen.
08 May 2011	Tilbury	6	Ulvik, Eidfjord, Flåm, Bergen.
14 May 2011	Tilbury	10	Invergordon, Kirkwall, Ullapool, Belfast, Dublin, St Mary's, St. Peter Port, Portland.
24 May 2011	Tilbury	8	Bergen, Molde, Åndalsnes, Geiranger, Flåm, Vik, Eidfjord.
01 June 2011	Tilbury	12	Copenhagen, Warnemünde, Tallinn, St. Petersburg, Helsinki, Stockholm, Kiel Canal.
13 June 2011	Tilbury	12	Floro, Leknes, Honningsvåg, Alta, Tromso, Svartisen Glacier, Åndalsnes, Bergen.
25 June 2011	Tilbury	12	Lerwick, Heimaey, Reykjavik, Isafjordur, Akureyri, Seydisfjordur, Tórshavn, Kirkwall.
07 July 2011	Tilbury	10	Invergordon, Kirkwall, Stornoway, Tobermory Dublin, St Mary's, St. Peter Port, Honfleur.
17 July 2011	Tilbury	15	Lerwick, Geiranger, Svartisen Glacier, Bodo, Honningsvåg, Klaksvik, Tórshavn, Kirkwall.
01 August 2011	Tilbury	12	Copenhagen, Warnemünde, Tallinn, St. Petersburg, Helsinki, Stockholm, Kiel Canal.
13 August 2011	Tilbury	7	Ulvik, Eidfjord, Flåm, Hellesylt, Geiranger, Bergen.
20 August 2011	Tilbury	7	Ulvik, Eidfjord, Flåm, Hellesylt, Geiranger, Bergen.
27 August 2011	Tilbury	3	Amsterdam, Antwerp.
30 August 2011	Tilbury	9	Invergordon, Stornoway, Tobermory Dublin, Cobh, Cherbourg, Honfleur.
08 September 2011	Tilbury	10	Ulvik, Eidfjord, Flåm, Vik, Oslo, Copenhagen, Kiel Canal, Amsterdam.
18 September 2011	Tilbury	11	Copenhagen, Warnemünde, Tallinn, St. Petersburg, Helsinki, Kiel Canal.
29 September 2011	Tilbury	11	Copenhagen, Warnemünde, Tallinn, St. Petersburg, Helsinki, Stockholm, Kiel Canal.
10 October 2011	Tilbury	16	Lisbon, Tangier, Port Mahon, Ajaccio, Livorno, Villefranche, Barcelona, Gibraltar, La Coruña.
26 October 2011	Tilbury	4	Rouen, Zeebrugge.
30 October 2011	Tilbury	13	Arrecife, Tenerife, Santa Cruz de la Palma, Funchal, Lisbon, La Coruña.
12 November 2011	Tilbury		**Final arrival of the 2011 cruise season.**
			DOCKING PERIOD
03 December 2011	Tilbury	4	Amsterdam, Zeebrugge, Antwerp.
08 December 2011	Tilbury	3	Amsterdam, Antwerp.
11 December 2011	Tilbury	2	Antwerp.
17 December 2011	Tilbury	3	Antwerp, Amsterdam.
20 December 2011	Tilbury	14	Vigo, Lisbon, Santa Cruz de la Palma, Tenerife, Arrecife, Funchal, Leixoes.
03 January 2012	Tilbury	45	Amsterdam, Lisbon, Funchal, Mindelo, Icoaraci, MacapáAlmeirim, Alto do Chao, Parintins, Manaus, Boca da Valéria, Santarem, Île du Salut, St. Georges, Mayreau, St. John's, Castries, Bridgetown, Horta, Ponta Delgada.
17 February 2012	Tilbury	14	Amsterdam, Svartisen Glacier, Svolvaer, Narvik, Tromso, Alta, Bergen.
02 March 2012	Tilbury	14	Amsterdam, Molde, Svartisen Glacier, Narvik, Leknes, Tromso, Alta, Bergen.
16 March 2012	Tilbury	14	Amsterdam, Molde, Svartisen Glacier, Harstad, Narvik, Tromso, Alta, Alesund, Bergen.
30 March 2012	Tilbury	3	Amsterdam, Antwerp.
02 April 2012	Tilbury	8	Honfleur, Le Verdon, Brest, St Peter Port.
10 April 2012	Tilbury	7	Cherbourg, Kinsale, Cobh, Belfast, Liverpool.
17 April 2012	Tilbury	6	Ulvik, Eidfjord, Flåm, Bergen.
23 April 2012	Tilbury	9	Invergordon, Tobermory, Dublin, Cobh, Honfleur.
02 May 2012	Tilbury	2	Antwerp.
05 May 2012	Tilbury	1	Tyne.
06 May 2012	Tyne	7	Ulvik, Eidfjord, Bergen, Flåm, Stavanger.
13 May 2012	Tyne	10	Honfleur, St Helier, St Mary's, Milford Haven, Belfast, Tobermory, Kirkwall, Invergordon.
23 May 2012	Tyne	5	Kirkwall, Stornoway, Ullapool, Invergordon. Leith.
28 May 2012	Leith	9	London Tilbury, Portsmouth, St Mary's Cardiff, Belfast, Douglas.
06 June 2012	Leith	12	Copenhagen, Warnemünde, Tallinn, St. Petersburg, Helsinki, Stockholm, Kiel Canal.
18 June 2012	Leith	8	Hellesylt, Åndalsnes, Olden, Skjolden, Bergen, Kirkwall.
26 June 2012	Leith	12	Molde, Åndalsnes, Leknes, Honningsvåg, Tromso, Hellesylt, Rosyth, Tilbury.
08 July 2012	Tilbury	12	Cobh, Glengariff, Galway, Killybegs, Greencastle, Douglas, Belfast, Leith.

20 July 2012	Tilbury	10	Invergordon, Kirkwall, Tobermory Dublin, St Mary's, St. Peter Port, Honfleur.
30 July 2012	Tilbury	12	Kiel Canal, Tallinn, St. Petersburg, Helsinki, Stockholm, Copenhagen, Oslo.
11 August 2012	Tilbury	15	La Coruña, Horta, Praia, Funchal, Leixoes.
26 August 2012	Tilbury	7	Ulvik, Eidfjord, Flåm, Hellesylt, Bergen.
02 September 2012	Tilbury	9	Invergordon, Ullapool, Tobermory Dublin, St Mary's, St. Helier, Honfleur.
11 September 2012	Tilbury	9	Gijón, Le Verdon, Brest, St Mary's, St Peter Port, Honfleur.
20 September 2012	Tilbury	3	Antwerp, Amsterdam.
23 September 2012	Tilbury	12	Warnemünde, Tallinn, St. Petersburg, Helsinki, Nynashamn, Kiel Canal.
05 October 2012	Tilbury	5	Amsterdam, Honfleur, Rouen, Antwerp.
10 October 2012	Tilbury	14	Lisbon, Tangier, Malaga, Cartagena, Palma, Valencia, Gibraltar, La Coruña.
27 October 2012	Tilbury	2	Amsterdam.
29 October 2012	Tilbury		**Final arrival of the 2012 cruise season.**
			DOCKING PERIOD
16 December 2012	Tilbury	3	Antwerp, Amsterdam.
20 December 2012	Tilbury	14	Vigo, Lisbon, Puerto Rosario, Las Palmas, Santa Cruz de la Palma, Funchal, Leixoes.
03 January 2013	Tilbury	42	Amsterdam, Lisbon, Funchal, Mindelo, Santarem, Boca da Valeria, Manaus, Parintins, Alto do Chao, Macapá, Île du Salut, St. Georges, Kingstown, Castries, Bridgetown, Horta, Ponta Delgada.
14 February 2013	Tilbury	14	Amsterdam, Alesund, Svartisen Glacier, Narvik, Alta, Tromso, Sortland, Åndalsnes, Bergen.
28 February 2013	Tilbury	14	Amsterdam, Alesund, Svartisen Glacier, Narvik, Alta, Tromso, Sortland, Antwerp.
14 March 2013	Antwerp		**Cruise cancelled for unscheduled shipyard repair period.**
			REPAIR PERIOD
31 March 2013	Tilbury	7	Amsterdam, Antwerp, Cherbourg, St Mary's, Honfleur.
07 April 2013	Tilbury	9	Invergordon, Stornoway, Tobermory, Dublin, Honfleur.
16 April 2013	Tilbury	6	Ulvik, Eidfjord, Flåm, Bergen.
22 April 2013	Tilbury	6	Ulvik, Eidfjord, Flåm, Bergen.
28 April 2013	Tilbury	7	Eidfjord, Flåm, Skjolden, Bergen.
05 May 2013	Tilbury	12	Copenhagen, Warnemünde, Tallinn, St. Petersburg, Helsinki, Stockholm, Kiel Canal.
17 May 2013	Tilbury	8	Eidfjord, Odda, GeirangerFlåm, Bergen.
25 May 2013	Tilbury	1	Leith.
26 May 2013	Leith	5	Tórshavn, Stornoway, Kirkwall.
31 May 2013	Leith	12	Copenhagen, Warnemünde, Tallinn, St. Petersburg, Helsinki, Stockholm, Kiel Canal.
12 June 2013	Leith	7	Flåm, Olden, Geiranger, Bergen, Kirkwall.
19 June 2013	Leith	11	Kirkwall, Heimaey, Reykjavik, Isafjordur, Akureyri, Seydisfjordur, Klaksvik, Kollafjordur, Lerwick.
30 June 2013	Leith	13	Molde, Åndalsnes, Tromso, Honningsvåg, Longyearbyen, NyAlesund, Tórshavn, Kirkwall.
13 July 2013	Leith	1	Tilbury.
14 July 2013	Tilbury	12	Bergen, Olden, Leknes, Honningsvåg, Tromso, Åndalsnes, Stavanger.
26 July 2013	Tilbury	9	Invergordon, Stornoway, Tobermory Dublin, St Mary's, St. Peter Port, Honfleur.
04 August 2013	Tilbury	12	Kirkwall, Heimaey, Reykjavik, Isafjordur, Akureyri, Seydisfjordur, Tórshavn, Lerwick.
16 August 2013	Tilbury	8	Eidfjord, Flåm, Gudvangen, Fjaerland, Balestrand, Olden, Bergen.
24 August 2013	Tilbury	12	Copenhagen, Warnemünde, Tallinn, St. Petersburg, Helsinki, Stockholm, Kiel Canal.
05 September 2013	Tilbury	10	Invergordon, Kirkwall, Stornoway, Tobermory, Dublin, St Mary's, St. Peter Port, Honfleur.
15 September 2013	Tilbury	6	Eidfjord, Flåm, Bergen.
21 September 2013	Tilbury	12	Copenhagen, Warnemünde, Tallinn, St. Petersburg, Helsinki, Nynashamn, Kiel Canal.
03 October 2013	Tilbury	3	Ghent, Amsterdam.
06 October 2013	Tilbury	14	Eidfjord, Olden, Leknes, Alta, Honningsvåg, Tromso, Narvik, Åndalsnes, Bergen.
20 October 2013	Tilbury	12	Copenhagen, Warnemünde, Tallinn, St. Petersburg, Helsinki.
03 November 2013	Tilbury	30	Ponta Delgada, St. John's, Gustavia, Philipsburg, Basseterre, Castries Kingstown, Bequia, Mayreau, Bridgetown, Horta.

03 December 2013	Tilbury		**Final arrivalof the 2013 cruise season.**
			DOCKING PERIOD
15 December 2013	Tilbury	3	Ghent, Amsterdam.
18 December 2013	Tilbury	2	Antwerp.
22 December 2013	Tilbury	14	La Coruña, Tenerife, Santa Cruz de la Palma, Funchal, Le Havre.
05 January 2014	Tilbury	42	Amsterdam, Lisbon, Funchal, Mindelo, Santarem, Boca da Valeria, Manaus, Parintins, Alto do Chao, Macapá, Île du Salut, St. Georges, Kingstown, Castries, Bridgetown, Horta, Ponta Delgada.
16 February 2014	Tilbury	14	Amsterdam, Alesund, Svartisen Glacier, Narvik, Alta, Tromso, Sortland, Åndalsnes, Bergen.
02 March 2014	Tilbury	14	Amsterdam, Alesund, Svartisen Glacier, Narvik, Alta, Tromso, Åndalsnes, Bergen.
16 March 2014	Tilbury	14	Amsterdam, Alesund, Alta, Tromso, Narvik, Åndalsnes, Bergen.
30 March 2014	Tilbury	5	Amsterdam, Rouen, Zeebrugge.
04 April 2014	Tilbury	9	Invergordon, Stornoway, Tobermory, Dublin, St Mary's, St Peter Port, Honfleur.
13 April 2014	Tilbury	6	Eidfjord, Flåm, Bergen.
19 April 2014	Tilbury	6	Ulvik, Eidfjord, Flåm, Bergen.
25 April 2014	Tilbury	7	Eidfjord, Flåm, Skjolden, Bergen.
02 May 2014	Tilbury	4	Amsterdam, Zeebrugge, Honfleur.
06 May 2014	Tilbury	12	Copenhagen, Warnemünde, Tallinn, St. Petersburg, Helsinki, Stockholm, Kiel Canal.
18 May 2014	Tilbury	6	Ulvik, Eidfjord, Flåm, Bergen.
24 May 2014	Tilbury	9	Invergordon, Stornoway, Tobermory, Dublin, St Mary's, St Peter Port, Honfleur.
02 June 2014	Tilbury	6	Zeebrugge, Portsmouth, Honfleur, Cherbourg.
08 June 2014	Tilbury	1	Tyne.
09 June 2014	Tyne	6	Tórshavn, Ullapool, Lerwick, Kirkwall.
15 June 2014	Tyne	12	Kiel Canal, Warnemünde, Tallinn, St. Petersburg, Helsinki, Stockholm, Copenhagen.
27 June 2014	Tyne	7	Geiranger, Åndalsnes, Olden, Skjolden.
04 July 2014	Tyne	14	Geiranger, Gravdal, Kirkenes, Murmansk, Honningsvåg, Tromso, Åndalsnes, Bergen.
18 July 2014	Tyne	1	Tilbury
19 July 2014	Tilbury	10	Invergordon, Kirkwall, Stornoway, Tobermory, Dublin, St Mary's, St Peter Port, Honfleur.
29 July 2014	Tilbury	8	Eidfjord, Flåm, Fjaerland, Balestrand, Olden, Bergen.
06 August 2014	Tilbury	3	Antwerp, Amsterdam.
09 August 2014	Tilbury	12	Tórshavn, Eskifjordur, Akureyri, Isafjordur, Reykjavik, Heimaey, Kirkwall.
21 August 2014	Tilbury	12	Copenhagen, Sassnitz, Tallinn, St. Petersburg, Helsinki, Stockholm, Kiel Canal.
02 September 2014	Tilbury	9	Invergordon, Stornoway, Tobermory, Dublin, St Mary's, St Peter Port, Honfleur.
11 September 2014	Tilbury	7	Ulvik, Eidfjord, Flåm, Geiranger, Bergen.
18 September 2014	Tilbury	3	Antwerp, Amsterdam.
21 September 2014	Tilbury	12	Copenhagen, Warnemünde, Tallinn, St. Petersburg, Helsinki, Nynashamn, Kiel Canal.
05 October 2014	Tilbury	2	Amsterdam.
07 October 2014	Tilbury	8	Amsterdam, Kiel Canal, Wismar, Helsingborg, Copenhagen, Oslo.
15 October 2014	Tilbury	12	Copenhagen, Warnemünde, Tallinn, St. Petersburg, Helsinki, Nynashamn, Kiel Canal.
27 October 2014	Tilbury	14	Eidfjord, Olden, Leknes, Tromso, Honningsvåg, Alta, Narvik, Åndalsnes, Bergen.
10 November 2014	Tilbury		**Final Arrival of the 2014 cruise season.**
			DOCKING PERIOD